The Four Stages of Spiritual Growth

Where Are You?
Where Are You Going?

Dirk Waren

Soaring Eagle Press

The Four Stages of Spiritual Growth

Copyright © 2015 by Dirk Waren

Unless otherwise indicated, all Scripture quotations are taken from the Holy Bible, New International Version®. NIV®. Copyright © 1973, 1978, 1984, 2011 by the International Bible Society. Used by permission of Zondervan Bible Publishers.

Many NIV citations are from the 2011 Revised edition.

Passages marked "NASB" are taken from the New American Study Bible. Copyright © 1977 by The Lockman Foundation.

Passages marked "KJV" are taken from the King James Version of the Bible.

Passages marked "NKJV" are taken from the New King James Version®. Copyright © 1979, 1980, 1982 by Thomas Nelson Inc.

Other cited translations are listed in the Bibliography.

All underlining and italics in scriptural citations are added by the author.

Pronominal references to Deity in this work are not always capitalized.

ISBN: 978-0692514214
PUBLISHED BY SOARING EAGLE PRESS
Youngstown

Printed in the United States of America

...until we all... become mature, attaining to the whole measure of the fullness of Christ.

~ Ephesians 4:13

CONTENTS

PART I

Understanding the Four Stages

PART I explains what the Four Stages of Spiritual Growth are and how they apply to the believer's walk with the LORD. This first part of the book starts basic and increases in detail chapter to chapter. By the time you're done with Chapter Four you'll fully understand the Four Stages.

PART II provides the tools you'll need to ensure continuing progress in the Four Stages.

Chapter One

Introduction to the Four Stages

Too many people tend to think that becoming a Christian is the end of their spiritual journey. In other words, Christianity's all about acquiring "fire insurance" and little beyond that. Yes, salvation from everlasting destruction is certainly an important benefit of the message of Christ, but **it's so much more**. Turning to the LORD in repentance and faith is merely the *beginning* of an incredible spiritual pilgrimage that starts with spiritual rebirth (Titus 3:5). This spectacular regeneration and reconciliation only signifies the end of the first stage of spiritual growth and not the end of one's spiritual journey altogether. In fact, it's the beginning of the first of three more glorious stages; and the last stage is nigh infinite. What am I talking about? I'm talking about the Four Stages of Spiritual Growth.

The First of the Four Stages of Spiritual Growth

The Bible shows that there are four basic stages of spiritual development. The first stage applies to unbelievers, as well as people who *say* they're believers but really aren't, like nominal "Christians"—Christians in name only. The other three stages apply to spiritually regenerated believers.

Why does the first stage apply to non-believers? Because it's a stage of spiritual separation from God. And, since God is the Fountain of Life from which all life flows (Psalm 36:9), being separate from the LORD means being separate from the ultimate source of life. This doesn't mean that unbelievers don't have a spirit or that they can't be spiritual to some degree, but rather that their spirit is dead to God and therefore unable to have a *relationship* in any genuine sense. To understand what this means, notice what Paul said to the Ephesian believers:

> **As for you, <u>you were dead in your transgressions and sins</u>, (2) in which you used to live when you followed the ways of this world and of the ruler of the kingdom of the air, the spirit who is now at work in those who are disobedient. (3) All of us also lived among them at one time, gratifying the cravings of our flesh and following its desires and thoughts. Like the rest, we were by nature deserving of wrath. (4) But because of his great love for us, God, who is rich in mercy, (5) <u>made us alive with Christ</u> even when we were <u>dead in transgressions</u>—it is by grace you have been saved.**
>
> **Ephesians 2:1-5**

Paul said that the Ephesian believers were once "dead in [their] transgressions and sins." This is a reference to their BC lives—*before* Christ. Being "dead in transgression" doesn't refer to being physically dead, of course, but rather *spiritually* dead, which means that the person's spirit is dead to their Creator and they can't connect or commune with Him in any intimate sense. This explains something Jesus said when he was praying to the Father:

> **"Righteous Father, though <u>the world does</u> <u>not know you</u>, <u>I know you</u>, and they know that you have sent me. (26) <u>I have made you known to</u> <u>them, and will continue to make you known</u> in order that the love you have for me may be in them and that I myself may be in them."**
>
> **John 17:25-26**

While Jesus knew the Father, he plainly declared that "the world does *not* know" God. This explains one of Christ's main purposes when he was on earth—to make the Creator known to people. Why? So that those who *believe* his message would know God like Jesus did and possess the same love of the Creator.

This shows that it's impossible for people to know God in any intimate sense apart from Christ's message. Sure, they can know *about* the Almighty, but they can't truly know Him. Moreover, it's impossible for spiritually dead people to do anything to change their condition and reconcile to the LORD *by their own efforts*. As such, no human-made religion can reconcile people to their Creator and grant forgiveness of sins or eternal life. This explains a statement Jesus made to his disciples when they asked him who could be saved. He responded:

> **"<u>With people it is impossible</u>, but not with God; for <u>all things are possible with God</u>."**
>
> **Mark 10:27**

Eternal salvation and everything that goes with it—reconciliation with the LORD, the forgiveness of sins and acquisition of eternal life—are only available through God and not human religion, including religious "Christianity," which isn't actual Christianity. These wonderful things are available exclusively from God through the gospel, which explains why 'gospel' literally means "good news." Actually it's not just good news, it's *totally awesome news!* Notice what the gospel of Christ does for people:

> …**because of his great love for us, God, who is rich in mercy, (5)** <u>made us alive with Christ</u> **even when we were** <u>dead in transgressions</u>—**it is by grace** [God's favor] **you have been saved.**
>
> **Ephesians 2:4-5**

This is the gospel, the 'good news': Because of God's "great love" and rich mercy we can be saved from eternal death by the LORD's favor (grace) and be "made alive with Christ even when… dead in transgressions"! You see? Christianity's all about being set free of spiritual death and its cause—sin and the sinful nature—and being made spiritually alive. When a person experiences this they are automatically transferred from STAGE ONE spirituality to STAGE TWO, which is merely the *beginning* of one's awesome journey with the awesome Fountain of Life—the LORD.

"In the Darkness"

The apostle John referred to STAGE ONE as being "in the darkness" as opposed to being "in the light," as shown here:

Anyone who claims to be in the light but hates a brother or sister is still <u>in the darkness</u>. (10) Anyone who loves their brother and sister lives <u>in the light</u>, and there is nothing in them to make them stumble. (11) But anyone who hates a brother or sister is <u>in the darkness</u> and walks around <u>in the darkness</u>. They do not know where they are going, because the darkness has blinded them.

1 John 2:9-11

Unbelievers are "in the darkness" simply because of their spiritual condition. While they have a spirit, it's dead to God and therefore they are unable to have a relationship. Since "God is light; in him there is no darkness" (1 John 1:5) those separate from God are in spiritual darkness. The aforementioned Psalm 36:9 says that the LORD is the Fountain of Life from which all life flows and "in His light [we] see light." Apart from the light of God we're "in the darkness."

The Three Stages of Christian Growth in the Bible

John fittingly follows up these references to being in STAGE ONE—"in the darkness"—with the other three stages of spiritual growth, which apply to believers; that is, those who are "in the light" through spiritual rebirth in Christ. John refers to these stages as "children," "young men" and "fathers":

(12) I am writing to you, dear <u>children</u>, because your sins have been forgiven on account of his name.

(13) I am writing to you, <u>fathers</u>, because you know him who is from the beginning.

I am writing to you, <u>young men</u>, because you have overcome the evil one.

(14) I write to you, dear <u>children</u>, because you know the Father.

I write to you, <u>fathers</u>, because you know him who is from the beginning.

I write to you, <u>young men</u>, because you are strong,

and the word of God lives in you, and you have overcome the evil one.

1 John 2:12-14

John wasn't being literal with his references to "children," "young men" and "fathers," but rather figurative. We know this for several reasons: **1.** Literal children wouldn't even read his epistle and wouldn't understand it if someone read it to them; **2.** not all mature believers reading his epistle (then or now) would be literal fathers—Paul's a good example—but *all* spiritually mature believers are *spiritual* fathers and mothers; **3.** Elsewhere in the Bible when Paul literally referred to segments of the congregation he did so in a more universal manner, as shown in Colossians 3:18-24 (i.e. wives, husbands, children, fathers and slaves); and **4.** John's references to "children," "young men" and "fathers" simply fits the Four Stage model, particularly since he referred to STAGE ONE three times in the previous three verses.

John's references to the Four Stages in 1 John 2:9-14 can be summed up as follows:

- "In the darkness" refers to the **spiritual darkness** of STAGE ONE where an unbeliever is separate from the light of God because his or her spirit is dead to Him.
- "Children" is a reference to the **boot camp fundamentalism** of STAGE TWO where the believer establishes a foundation. Unfortunately, too many Christians get stuck in this stage and never grow beyond it. They live and die as spiritual children.
- "Young men" refers to the **growing individualism and sense of freedom and adulthood** of STAGE THREE.
- "Fathers" is a reference to the **maturity and independence** of STAGE FOUR where believers naturally propagate.

We'll look at this powerful passage in more detail in Chapter Four.

Biblical References to Spiritual Growth

Let me reemphasize: Becoming a believer is not the end of our spiritual journey; it's merely the end of the first stage of spiritual development. As such, **there are constant references to growing spiritually in the Bible**. For instance, Jesus lamented that his disciples weren't further along than they were (Mark 9:17-29); the writer of Hebrews was astonished that the believers he was addressing weren't yet beyond the elementary stage (Hebrews 5:12-14); Peter likened new believers to "newborn babies" whom he encouraged to **"grow up** in [their] salvation" (1 Peter 2:2); he also gave specific details on how to **grow spiritually** (2 Peter 1:3-11); and Paul elaborated on what's necessary to **"become mature"** and to **"no longer be infants"** (Ephesians 4:11-16); not to mention he spoke of the view that all "mature" believers should have, which indicates that not all Christians are mature (Philippians 3:15). Furthermore, the Scriptures clearly show that there's supposed to be a *progression* to spiritual growth (Philippians 1:25). **If there's no progression something's wrong**.

So the idea that people's spiritual journey ends once they embrace the gospel is a myth, a lie straight from the kingdom of darkness. Think about it: The devil and filthy spirits *want* believers to accept this falsehood so they don't grow up and become a threat to their wicked kingdom!

M. Scott Peck's Version of the Four Stages

You may have heard of the "four stages of spiritual development," which were theorized by M. Scott Peck (1936-2005) and detailed in two of his books from the late 80s and early 90s.[1] Peck was essentially a non-sectarian Christian and formulated his theory based on another's work. As a psychiatrist, he developed his version of the Four Stages from a psychological viewpoint mixed with Christianity rather than purely a biblical one.

The Four Stages as relayed in this book, by contrast, are firmly rooted in biblical truth and Christian experience. For instance, Peck never cites the aforementioned biblical reference to the Four Stages in his works (1 John 2:9-14) so I'm assuming he wasn't aware that it is a reference to the Four Stages. As such, my version of the Four Stages is quite different than Peck's. While I give him credit for popularizing the theory and I acknowledge his insights on the topic, he didn't actually formulate the Four Stages; the Holy Spirit did via the God-breathed Scriptures. Furthermore, as a minister of God I naturally feel he deviated too much from scriptural truth, particularly by suggesting that a spiritually dead person—an unbeliever—could reach STAGE TWO, THREE and FOUR. They can in a substitutionary sense, but their inherent spiritual condition—being dead to God and unable to have a real

---

[1] Cited in the bibliography.

relationship—pins them down to STAGE ONE. We'll look at this further in <u>Chapter Three</u>.

I want to stress that I'm not a follower of Peck and don't know every jot and tittle of what he believed or taught and don't care to, but I found his writings on the Four Stages fascinating when I first read them in 2000. I discerned that he was on to something—something scriptural and very real—but it was clear that his secular studies tainted his understanding of the topic. The last time I remember reading any of his writings was circa 2001. So this book was written without referencing his works and similarities are based purely on memory. In short, this is my own take on the Four Stages of Spiritual Growth in light of what the Bible teaches.

Because the material in this book is rooted in scriptural truth rather than pop-psychology it isn't politically correct and will no doubt offend secularists and universalists who claim that— contrary to what the Bible says—spiritually un-regenerated people can genuinely know God and attain spiritual maturity. Again, this is only true in a limited pseudo-sense because of their spiritual condition—being separate from God and in dire need of spiritual regeneration (John 3:3,6). This doesn't mean they can't know *about* the Creator. Actually, all unbelievers know about God in the sense that they intrinsically know He exists since they have a spirit, whether they care to admit it or not, but their understanding is darkened (Ephesians 4:18). Nor does it mean that they can't catch a glimpse of God or desire to know the Almighty. In fact, anyone who moves up to the higher levels of STAGE ONE will surely experience both. So this book isn't suggesting that unsaved people can't move to higher stages in a substitutionary sense. Again, there are secular *substitutions* to STAGE TWO and STAGE THREE and even STAGE FOUR in a sense (we'll look at this further in <u>Chapter Three</u>), but this doesn't change the unbeliever's spiritual condition and their inability to genuinely know God. According to the Four Stages as relayed in the Holy Scriptures, they're still in

STAGE ONE—"in the darkness"—and therefore "dead in their transgressions."

Why this Book is Important to Your Spiritual Development

This book will help you see the biblical validity of the Four Stages of Spiritual Growth, which I'm confident you'll find fascinating and enlightening. In addition, it will help you see:

- **Where you are spiritually.**
- **Where you need to go.**
- And it will help you **locate where others are spiritually** so you can understand their position and relate to them accordingly.

Beyond this, PART II provides all the tools you'll need to grow spiritually. Needless to say, if you want to develop and mature spiritually this book is for YOU.

Chapter Two

Overview of the Four Stages

Let's now define and explain each of the Four Stages.

STAGE ONE: Separation from God / Chaos

This is the classic "sinner" stage where the individual is separate from God and therefore **in spiritual darkness**. At this stage people are in bondage to the flesh—the sinful nature—to one degree or another. Because people in this stage are separate from God and in spiritual darkness, you could also describe it as moral chaos. While morality is self-evident and universal, people in STAGE ONE, particularly the lower levels, are often so hardened in heart or tainted by their ungodly culture or sub-culture—whatever that might be—they're unable to discern the simplest of moral truths. This explains why the LORD referred to the Assyrian inhabitants of Nineveh as not being able to "tell their right hand from their left" (Jonah 4:11). We see this today where secularists argue that there's nothing inherently wrong with homosexuality when it's clear that the sexual organs simply don't line up for such a union. As such, they'll advocate children growing up in homes with "two daddies" or "two mommies." They're in such spiritual darkness they can't see the forest for the trees, morally speaking.[2]

As noted in the first chapter, I'm not saying that people in STAGE ONE don't have a spirit, since every human being has a spirit, but rather that their spirit is dead to God and therefore in need of regeneration.

STAGE TWO cannot occur until the individual is enlightened to his or her needy spiritual condition and turns to God via the good news of the gospel, which is called "the message of *reconciliation*" in Scripture (2 Corinthians 5:18-20). This awesome salvation comes through **repentance** and **faith** (Acts 20:21), which we'll address in Chapter Nine.

---

[2] Before someone rashly accuses me of being a "bigot," please keep this in mind: The Bible plainly teaches that "God so loved the world that he gave his one and only Son, that whoever believes in him shall not perish but have eternal life" (John 3:16). This includes homosexuals. Like all people, **the LORD loves them and has provided a way for them to escape the wages of sin—death—and obtain eternal life**. Is homosexuality wrong in God's eyes? Yes, but so is fornication, adultery, drunkard-ness, pomposity, hatred, strife, gossip, slander, religious hypocrisy and numerous other sins (see 1 Corinthians 6:9-10 & Galatians 5:19-21). The wages of all sin is death and God wants us to escape it through the gospel (Romans 6:23). You see, there's no discrimination—the LORD wants *all people across the board* to be set free from slavery to fleshly bondages. Christianity's all about freedom: "It is **for freedom** that Christ has set you free" (Galatians 5:1). Modern culture has embraced two **lies**: **1.** If you disapprove of someone's lifestyle it automatically means that you fear or hate them; and **2.** to truly love someone you must agree with everything they believe and do. Needless to say, this is absurd. I don't approve of practicing alcoholics, addicts and fornicators, but this doesn't mean I fear or hate them. I actively walk in love toward arrogant people, liars, adulterers and slanderers, but that doesn't mean I agree with their destructive behaviors. And by "walk in love" I don't just mean the gentle variety because sometimes "tough love" is in order, which includes sharing the awful truth about the wages of sin—eternal death.

STAGE TWO: Institutional / Fundamental

After reconciliation with God, the new believer will ideally join an assembly/ministry/sect. The group's oversight and biblical instruction provide the necessary structure for him or her. Hence the moral **chaos** of STAGE ONE transforms into **order** as the organization and God's Word provide protection and accountability for the convert, not to mention opportunities to learn, participate, serve, grow and eventually lead in some capacity, small or great.

STAGE TWO can be described as "fundamental" because those at this level become attached to the rules and doctrines of the organization, which the elders decree to be fundamental to their faith. Not surprisingly, STAGE TWO believers become discombobulated when these fundamentals are threatened, regardless of whether the "fundamentals" are true, false or somewhere in between. As such, those in this stage are "fundamentalists."

STAGE TWO is essentially **Christian boot camp**. It's a phase of spiritual immaturity where the believer is learning and growing. It's immature in the sense that the believer is typically *dependent* upon the group to maintain his or her spiritual status. Just as in military boot camp recruits need their drill instructors and the military institution or they'll revert back to their civilian ways, Christian converts are very dependent on their churches and elders without which they'll fall back into STAGE ONE.

Ideally, the new believer will be in STAGE TWO while simultaneously growing in STAGE THREE and STAGE FOUR, as shown here:

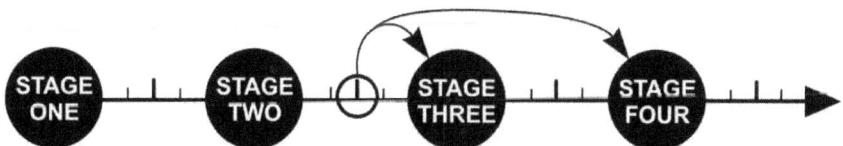

Unfortunately, this doesn't always happen. Sometimes believers get stuck in STAGE TWO, usually because the church or sect they hook up with is infected by legalism, which is sterile (counterfeit) "Christianity" and characterized by rigid sectarianism. When this occurs, the organization foolishly fosters a spirit of dependency in the believer rather than independency, bondage rather than freedom and weakness rather than strength. This is actually spiritual *abuse* because it harms or limits the believer's growth. Abuse, by the way, is the misuse of power.

STAGE THREE: Individual / Seeker

Healthy believers will grow as **individuals** and develop an identity separate from the organization of STAGE TWO. They'll start to question doctrines of their group that don't really gel with the Scriptures or make sense. They'll seek truth—*reality*—beyond the limitations of their sect and elders; that is, if they sense they're in error in one area or another. This is good because it's impossible for error to set people free, even if it's disguised as "truth" by one's church or pastor. Only the truth sets free, as Jesus taught, and truth is reality—the way it really is (John 8:31-32). Also, as believers develop in STAGE THREE they will cultivate discernment to spiritual abuse and will not tolerate it, which explains why **weak "pastors" try to keep individuals in STAGE TWO**. I put "pastors" in quotes here because *real* pastors passionately desire for believers to grow spiritually.

Now, just because believers in STAGE THREE discover error or abuse in their group it doesn't mean they'll automatically leave. They'll likely stay and do their part to help correct any problems, but this depends on many factors. Such as: How deeply involved are they in the group? What about their families and close friends? How severe is the error or abuse? What do they discern the Holy Spirit leading them to do? How long have they been trying to help without any appreciable change?

In STAGE THREE believers may find themselves questioning beliefs, especially ones that don't really jibe with the Scriptures. They may even question the reliability of the Bible or their faith in God, His existence and goodness. This happened to me after sixteen years of being a steadily growing believer. I found myself questioning *everything* I learned about Christendom over the course of a summer, but this drove me to seek the truth with greater accuracy and so it was ultimately a good thing. These kinds of experiences in STAGE THREE are simply growth pangs because it's where believers develop as free-thinking individuals. They'll typically question the official doctrines of their sect and the image of God they're sect has painted. This is actually a positive thing because it helps believers decipher what's true and not true in their group and it subsequently weeds out error. It leads to them believing something because they're convinced of it and not just because their pastor/church/sect told them it was true. In short, it leads to going deeper in the LORD.

Another good thing about this is that it helps believers discern unhealthy fellowships or sects and leave if necessary. The reason legitimate believers stay in legalistic or abusive ministries is because they're stuck in STAGE TWO. Anyone who truly enters into STAGE THREE, by contrast, will not stay in such a ministry. However, this isn't to say that God won't call someone in STAGE FOUR to go to such a group and (try to) minister life to them, at least for a season.

Because of this questioning element of STAGE THREE, it *can* be an uncertain or unpredictable stage in the Christian pilgrimage. I've known people who were believers for many years in STAGE TWO, but as they (seemingly) segued into STAGE THREE they totally fell away from God and faith. Usually the signs were there that this was where they were heading. They failed to "guard their heart as the wellspring of life" (Proverbs 4:23) and, as a result, let things enter in that eventually took their hearts away from their pure devotion to the LORD. Jesus said that the Word can be prevented from bearing fruit in people's lives if they allow it to be choked by life's anxieties and the pursuit of wealth or pleasure, including the pleasures of the flesh (Luke 8:14). Guarding one's heart is a matter of wisdom and believers make a big mistake when they allow negative things to enter in, which eventually take them away from their "first love" (Revelation 2:4-5). When believers who do this move away from the protective care of their group in STAGE TWO they can't handle it and thus revert back to STAGE ONE.

Thankfully, STAGE THREE doesn't end this way for those who *genuinely* seek God and persist rather than use STAGE THREE as an excuse to backtrack to STAGE ONE. Let me rephrase that: Foolish believers use STAGE THREE as an excuse to revert back to STAGE ONE and, as such, it's not really STAGE THREE (that is, *if* it's a lasting condition). In reality they didn't *progress* to STAGE THREE, they *regressed* to STAGE ONE.

STAGE THREE can be difficult due to the inherent growth pangs, but it's a necessary and important stage of growth in the believer's odyssey. It's a part of the maturation process where believers develop their sense of individuality apart from the group. STAGE THREE motivates them to seek out the truth for more certainty and accuracy, not to mention clarify their objectives. Without STAGE THREE believers will be stuck in STAGE TWO and therefore cannot move on to STAGE FOUR.

STAGE FOUR: Knowing God (Intimately)

STAGE FOUR is the stage where believers develop a living *relationship* with God rather than just knowing about Him. This is the goal of Christianity and explains why the gospel of Christ is called the "message of reconciliation" (2 Corinthians 5:18-20). It also explains something profound Paul said:

> **What is more, I consider <u>everything a loss</u> because of the surpassing worth of <u>knowing Christ Jesus my Lord</u>, for whose sake I have lost all things. I consider them <u>garbage</u>, that I may gain Christ (9) and be found in him, not having a righteousness of my own that comes from the law, but that which is through faith in Christ— the righteousness that comes from God on the basis of faith. (10) <u>I want to know Christ</u>—yes, to <u>know</u> the power of his resurrection and participation in his sufferings, becoming like him in his death, (11) and so, somehow, attaining to the resurrection from the dead.**
>
> **Philippians 3:8-11**

Believers who progress to STAGE FOUR increasingly consider everything a loss compared to *knowing* the Lord. Why? Because everything else essentially becomes "garbage" by comparison. They've genuinely tasted of the LORD (Psalm 34:8) and therefore want to *know* God above all else, not just know *about* Him or know Him from a distance. They want to walk in the power of the Spirit and experience the awesome newness of life Christ offers, not just observe others walking in it (Hebrews 6:5 & Romans 6:4).

I don't want to be taken wrong here because, to one degree or another, all genuine believers know God because they've been reconciled to Him through the message of Christ. It's just that believers who "graduate" to STAGE FOUR know the LORD in a more intimate and infinite sense. STAGE TWO believers, by contrast, only relate to God as their parent who has to lovingly monitor them. The Galatian believers during the mid-1st century, for instance, were largely STAGE TWO because they didn't even know enough to recognize legalists who "bewitched" them with their legalism and false doctrines. Notice what Paul says about them:

> But **now that you know God—or rather are known by God**—how is it that you are turning back to those weak and miserable forces? Do you wish to be enslaved by them all over again?
>
> **Galatians 4:9**

Paul says that the Galatians knew God, but then adds important exposition: It was more correct to say they were known *by* God. This was a covert rebuke to the Galatians who were ignorant and foolish enough to allow counterfeit believers—the legalistic Judaizers—to infiltrate their churches and lead them astray (Galatians 3:1 & 5:4). My point is that the Galatians didn't know God in an intimate sense. They were rather known by God and, as such, were still in STAGE TWO. We'll look at this further in Chapter Four.

STAGE FOUR is Enlightenment, Independence and Strength

STAGE FOUR is a stage of **enlightenment**, **independence** and **strength**. Let's look at all three:

STAGE FOUR is **enlightenment** because the believer is in direct communion with God rather than relying on a pastor or elder to pray for them. In STAGE FOUR this communion becomes a 24/7 thing where the believer is in constant connection with their Creator, which is what Paul was referring to when he mentioned "praying without ceasing" (1 Thessalonians 5:17 ESV/KJV). Enlightenment in this manner includes the constant awareness of God's presence via the Holy Spirit and also the awesomeness, beauty and mystery of actually knowing the LORD. Those stuck in STAGE TWO, by contrast, only have an inkling of this and basically view God as a big cop in the sky. This is an *outward* perspective of God and it's frankly an Old Testament mentality. The New Testament, by contrast, emphasizes the believer's spiritual regeneration and the indwelling empowerment of the Holy Spirit—God is *within us!* See Titus 3:5, 1 Corinthians 3:16 and Ephesians 1:19.

STAGE FOUR is also **independence** from bondage to the error and corruption that often comes with the institution of STAGE TWO. Please read that again and chew on it. This isn't to say that the church/sect/pastors that believers are hooked up with in STAGE TWO are always bad or that they're all bad—not at all—they're usually good, depending on the quality of the leadership and organization, but error and abuse come with the territory of people and groups, even legitimate Christian churches and sects. It's just the way it is.

Furthermore, STAGE FOUR is **independence** from the uncertainty of STAGE THREE. How so? In STAGE FOUR believers know God personally. They've "tasted and seen that the LORD is good" (Psalm 34:8). As such, it's impossible for someone to convince them that God doesn't exist because they personally walk with God daily. This isn't to say, of course, that believers in STAGE FOUR are exempt from falling from faith, only that it's much harder for them to fall than those in STAGE

TWO or THREE. Why? Because they're actually walking with God 24/7.

This combination of enlightenment and independence makes for **strong** believers. Genuine believers in STAGE THREE are strong too due to the biblical foundation established in STAGE TWO, not to mention the personal discipline they've developed, but those in STAGE FOUR are even stronger because they're more spiritually mature. They *know* God beyond just Daddy who provides goodies and therefore increasingly *know* their calling. They don't just sacrifice 10% of their finances as a tithe, they're whole lives are "living sacrifices" when they wake up in the morning (Romans 12:1). Because they discern and fulfill God's will on both minor and major levels they become a threat to the enemy's kingdom, which naturally draws attack. This includes opposition from people at the lower stages of growth, including quasi-believers and legalists, like the Pharisees during Jesus' earthly ministry. Of course, there are modern "Pharisees" all around us; they just don't go by that moniker.

Furthermore, those in STAGE FOUR become increasingly **independent** of the need of others in order to stay tight with God and fulfill their calling. What I'm saying is that believers in STAGE TWO and even STAGE THREE will fall back into STAGE ONE without the service, support and encouragement of fellow believers, particularly in the context of quality church services, but believers firmly walking in STAGE FOUR don't need others to walk free of the pitfalls of the flesh and legalism. They don't need pastors to motivate them to spiritual disciplines, like prayer, study, worship, fasting, etc. Don't get me wrong, Paul was encouraged and blessed by other believers, and so should every Christian, but Paul performed spiritual disciplines and fulfilled his calling *without* people over him compelling him to do so. Jesus did the same and every Christian is called to follow their godly examples (1 Corinthians 11:1 & John 12:26). Needless to say, every believer should aspire to this level of spirituality. The ones who don't *aren't* spiritually mature.

By the way, I'm not saying that believers in STAGE FOUR shouldn't attend church services. Going to healthy Christian gatherings is always good, regardless of where you are spiritually. But those in STAGE FOUR will often lead their own ministries within other ministries or pioneer their own, whether within an existing camp or independently.

In light of all this, STAGE FOUR is clearly a stage of **strength.** Of course, there is a downside: "Higher levels bigger devils." But those in STAGE FOUR can handle the increased attacks and their intensity because, again, they're tight with the LORD. A good scriptural example is Paul who endured great persecutions while he traveled the eastern Mediterranean area, starting and overseeing numerous fellowships. Check out Paul's incredible list of sufferings in 2 Corinthians 11:23-28 sometime. It includes hardships like frequent imprisonment; severe flogging; several near-fatal experiences, like being beaten with rods, stoned, shipwrecked, adrift at sea, attacks by bandits, persecution from legalists and false believers; not to mention the labor, toil and sacrifices of serious ministry. In addition, he experienced hunger, thirst and knew what it was like to be cold and naked during his long travels. **Someone in STAGE TWO or STAGE THREE could never endure such hardships without falling away**, but those in the higher levels of STAGE FOUR can, just as Paul did.

Levels within the Stages

Take another look at the Four Stage diagram and you'll notice that there are levels within each stage:

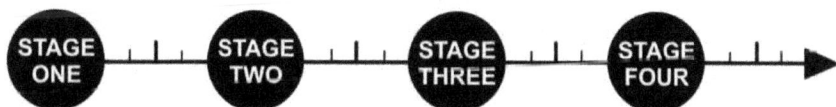

As people go further in the stage they're in they'll gain a greater foothold in the forthcoming stage. For instance, people in the higher levels of STAGE TWO are already developing the qualities of STAGE THREE and consequently are developing as free-thinking individuals separate from the supervision of the group of STAGE TWO. They're also presumably developing qualities of STAGE FOUR.

The Bible refers to this maturation from one level to the next in terms of going "from strength to strength" or "glory to glory" (Psalm 84:4,5,7: & 2 Corinthians 3:18).

Even unbelievers at the higher end of STAGE ONE have a finger in STAGE TWO in the sense that they're primed to receive the message of Christ and reconcile with the Creator. Unbelievers at the lower end of STAGE ONE, by contrast, have zero interest in God or the gospel because their hearts are hardened to both. As people move up the levels of each stage their hearts become softer toward God and His Word. They increasingly seek Him and the good thing about this is revealed in this biblical axiom:

> **Come near to God and <u>he will</u> come near to you.**
>
> **James 4:8**

Anyone who genuinely draws near to the LORD, God will draw closer to him/her.

You'll notice in the diagram that STAGE FOUR ends with an arrow proceeding forward. Why? Because there's no end to this stage. The growth of believers in STAGE FOUR depends upon how close they are to God and, since there are no limits to the infinite Almighty, there's no limit to one's growth in relation to Him.

Chapter Three

Insights on
the Four Stages

Now that we know what the Four Stages are, let's consider further insights about each stage and how they relate.

Getting Stuck in STAGE TWO

As noted in the previous chapter, believers in STAGE TWO should simultaneously be growing in STAGE THREE and FOUR. In other words, as believers grow in the realm of **Christian community** (STAGE TWO), they should also be growing as an **individual** (STAGE THREE) and in their **relationship with God** (STAGE FOUR). Healthy believers always have a finger, hand or foot in the next stage, as well as the next level of the stage they're in.

But what of those who get stuck in STAGE TWO? These are people who fail to develop spiritually as individuals and in relationship with their Creator. Instead, the institution they're involved with—their church fellowship and its camp—replaces both. This isn't good because, in essence, the institution itself becomes their God. They become "sheeple"—mindless automatons dedicated to perpetuating the machine of the institution, their "god." This explains why those stuck in STAGE TWO become rigid sectarians who eye outsiders suspiciously and get irate when someone merely questions the legitimacy of the rules and doctrines of their group. Why do they do this? Because the institution has taken the place of the LORD. You'll see this with cults like the Jehovah's False Witnesses, but Mainline, Evangelical and Charismatic churches can be infected by the same spirit. It's really a form of idolatry.

Too many pastors are weak (or even counterfeits) in that they encourage the pastoral dependency of STAGE TWO and are threatened by those trying to move into the next two stages. Instead of thinking in terms of apprehending *new* disciples—converts— they think in terms of "holding on" to their current fold by intentionally keeping them in the dependent stage of STAGE TWO. They don't want to "lose" them, not realizing that losing them is the best thing for them because they would grow up spiritually, becoming "young men" (STAGE THREE) and "fathers" (STAGE FOUR). As a minister I know puts it: "My job is to become *unnecessary* in the life of the believer."

The Foundational Importance of STAGE TWO

The above shouldn't be misinterpreted to mean that I look down on STAGE TWO because this isn't the case at all. STAGE TWO is absolutely strategic to a healthy spiritual journey. It's the stage where believers set a foundation for their lifelong spiritual walk and develop discipline with the service and supervision of more mature believers. It's where they learn the ropes of basic Christianity and cultivate the character necessary to progress to maturity.

Consider this example from the Bible:

> **If you point these things out to the brothers and sisters, you will be a good minister of Christ Jesus, nourished on the truths of the faith and of the good teaching that you have followed.**
>
> .   **1 Timothy 4:6**

Paul is talking to young pastor Timothy and he says "If you point these things out to the brothers and sisters, you will be a good minister of Christ Jesus." Point what things out? The doctrinal truths he shared up to this point in his epistle, as well as warnings of various false teachings, like forbidding believers to marry and making them abstain from certain foods (see verses 3-5). Look again at the phrase "If you point these things out to the brothers and sisters..." The key Greek word here is *hupotithémi (hoop-ot-ITH-ay-mee)*, which is a compound word. *Hupo* means "underneath" and *tithémi* means "to place, position or lay a foundation." So Paul's instructing Timothy to **lay a foundation** for the believers under his care based on the Word of God he just gave him. If Timothy does this he will be a "good minister of Christ Jesus." The point is that **good ministers lay a quality foundation for believers in STAGE TWO because they know the rest of their spiritual walk depends upon it**.

Paul goes on to describe Timothy as "nourished on the truths of the faith and of the good teaching that you have followed." This is why Timothy was such an effective minister and why Paul entrusted him with missions of great importance, including the governing of churches. What was the foundation of this success? Timothy was "nourished on the truths of the faith and... good teaching." This refers to the spiritual foundation that was set in Timothy's life. Who laid this strong foundation? Certainly Timothy's grandmother and mother, Lois and Eunice when Timothy was a kid (2 Timothy 1:5), but also Paul himself as he later became Paul's disciple and co-worker. Paul was sure to lay a solid understructure for Timothy and that's why he was now being used so greatly in the LORD's service.

Don't Skip Out on STAGE TWO!

We talked about believers getting stuck in STAGE TWO, which isn't good, but even worse are those who try to skip STAGE TWO and jump ahead to STAGE THREE. This includes prematurely leaving STAGE TWO. Believers who do this make a huge mistake. Why? Because they fail to set a solid foundation and without a good foundation you can't build properly. Jesus talked about this:

> Therefore <u>everyone who hears these words of mine and puts them into practice is like a wise man who built his house on the rock.</u> (25) The rain came down, the streams rose, and the winds blew and beat against that house; yet it did not fall, because it had its foundation on the rock. (26) But everyone who hears these words of mine and does not put them into practice is like a foolish man who built his house on sand. (27) The rain came down, the streams rose, and the winds blew and beat against that house, and it fell with a great crash."
>
> **Matthew 7:24-27**

Who is Jesus speaking of when he says "everyone who hears these words of mine and puts them into practice is like a wise man who built his house on the rock"? He's talking about those in STAGE TWO because that's the stage where believers are taught the Word of God and learn to put it into practice with the help of more mature believers. Those who cultivate the discipline necessary to regularly practice the word of God—even in the face of temptation or trial—develop character. All this occurs in STAGE TWO. Believers who do this are "wise," as Jesus said, because they "build [their] house on the rock," meaning they lay a firm foundation for their spiritual journey, which the oncoming storms *can't* destroy.

Foolish believers, by contrast, fail to develop the discipline and character necessary to put God's Word into practice. So, as Jesus elsewhere said, "in the time of testing they fall away" (Luke 8:13). Please understand that trouble or persecution will automatically come to the believer after they've received the Word. This includes the salvation message of Christ (Matthew 13:21). Believers who fail to develop discipline with the feeding, supervision and example of ministers during STAGE TWO **will not be able to stand in the time of testing**. Doing so is like building a structure on sand. When the storms come the structure can't handle it and therefore falls. This is what happens to believers who try to skip STAGE TWO or leave it prematurely.

So it's vital to develop discipline and character in STAGE TWO in order to handle the independence, temptations and risk of STAGE THREE, as well as the hardships and increased persecution of STAGE FOUR. Those who try to skip STAGE TWO will either fall back to STAGE ONE completely or have one foot perpetually manacled to STAGE ONE, which of course will severely limit their walk with the Lord. Let me give two examples:

One young guy I knew for a number of months was a genuine believer with wide-eyed potential. I was able to spend some quality time with him on numerous occasions, discussing

God and biblical topics at length, but then he left the area and I didn't see him for over a decade. When I finally got back in touch with him I discovered that he had been struggling with drunkardness & pill-popping and, worse, was in trouble with the law. He explained to me that he never settled down with a church/ministry because he believed all churchgoers were "hypocrites," which I found incredibly ironic in light of the fact that he had been engaging in substance abuse and criminal activity and yet he was a confessing believer. The truth was that he used the "all Christians are hypocrites" lie as an excuse to avoid the time & effort requisite to STAGE TWO and waddle in the mud of STAGE ONE. The good news is that his serious problems were a wake-up call and, the last I talked with him, he was diligently studying the Bible and seeking the LORD. He was back to the beginning level of STAGE TWO where he'll (hopefully) establish the necessary foundation and develop the character he'll need to move on to STAGE THREE and FOUR.

Another example: a minister I knew was thoroughly in STAGE THREE with a finger in STAGE FOUR. Sometimes it was fascinating talking to him and hearing his spiritual insights, but other times it was like hanging out with a slab of flesh. I'm not being mean; just honest. His constant bloviating, boasting and gossip were so nauseating I had to cut ties with him. Although he was very independent and self-motivated—signs of STAGE THREE—with leadership qualities and sometimes amazing insights from God's Word—signs of STAGE FOUR (or, at least, higher level STAGE THREE)—it was clear that he didn't work out some fleshly kinks on his Christian sojourn. He told me of a ministry where his spiritual foundation was set but he obviously didn't spend enough time in this stage. If he did he wouldn't have been displaying the fleshly problems I witnessed. The good news is that I heard from him recently and he was hooked up with an assembly where he was fixing his foundation through some great ministry of the Word (Acts 6:1-4). Moreover, the LORD had severely disciplined him and so he was humbled and dedicated to producing fruit. Praise God!

While these two examples reveal the folly of skipping STAGE TWO or prematurely leaving it, they also show that **1.** just because someone unwisely tries to skip STAGE TWO it doesn't mean s/he can't go back and do it right; and **2.** just because someone prematurely leaves STAGE TWO it doesn't mean s/he can't go back and finish their foundation.

What about those with a Flawed Foundation?

What about those who go through STAGE TWO and develop a flawed spiritual foundation due to false doctrine,[3] legalistic leaders, bad examples or some combination? The good news is that you can always go back and fix your foundation, which is great, of course, but there are a number of things to consider.

While it's understandable that believers regard the church/sect they hook up with in STAGE TWO as the "one true church" in that they feel their group is right about everything and does everything perfectly pleasing to the Lord, this is never the case no matter how excellent the ministry is. As such, **it's *always* necessary for believers to go back and fix their foundation after moving on to STAGE THREE and FOUR when they acquire more accurate information**. In the natural we repair the foundations to structures all the time and it's no different in the realm of the spirit. Remember, each of us is a temple of God (1 Corinthians 3:16) and together we also form the "house of God" (1 Peter 4:17, 1 Timothy 3:15, Hebrews 3:6 & 1 Peter 2:5).

---

[3] "False doctrine" includes teachings/beliefs that are only partially true and therefore are partially false or, at best, inadequate.

Some people go through STAGE TWO and the foundation that's laid is so flawed it needs extensive repairs; or it's severely incomplete and needs finishing. Sometimes their foundation is so amiss it needs redone altogether and it's amazing in such cases when the believer's faith isn't utterly destroyed by the lousy groundwork. This shows the importance of setting a quality foundation in STAGE TWO and why God holds ministers accountable to the job they do, as shown in 1 Corinthians 3:5-17. Make no mistake, ministers who harm or destroy believers with faulty "ministry" and false teaching will have to answer to the Almighty.

One of the reasons it's necessary to build a quality foundation in STAGE TWO is that it influences you for years to come and often the rest of your life. I know people who won't change their view on an important doctrine even though there's strong scriptural support disproving it because it goes against what they were (wrongly) taught in STAGE TWO. This indicates immaturity. While they may be in STAGE THREE of FOUR to some degree, such an immature mindset shows that they still have a foot in STAGE TWO.

The awesome news I want to drive home here is that a bad spiritual foundation doesn't mean a believer is condemned to being "damaged goods" for life. This is a lie and don't you believe it! You can always go back and repair flawed groundwork or even redo the foundation altogether, as necessary. We *all* have to do this to some degree no matter what church/sect from which we spring.

Laying a Good Foundation (STAGE TWO) and Inspecting It (STAGE THREE)

When I became a believer and consequently entered STAGE TWO I visited several churches looking to establish the groundwork for the rest of my spiritual walk. I didn't stay overly

long in churches that had weak feeding (sermons/teachings) or
were just plain sterile for one reason or another. I kept looking
until I found a ministry that I knew would help lay a quality
foundation and stayed there for a whole decade. To this day I'm
exceedingly grateful for this particular ministry (which is still
going strong), but after ten years a solid biblical understructure
was established in my life and the LORD moved me onward. Some
people will stay in their foundational group/sect, depending on the
Holy Spirit's leading, but I was led to move on.

As awesome as the foundation was that I received in that
ministry, it wasn't perfect and I had to go back in the ensuing years
to make repairs. This is an important part of STAGE THREE—
inspecting the legitimacy of the foundation set in STAGE TWO
and making the necessary repairs or adjustments in light of what
the Bible clearly and consistently teaches (keeping in mind that
we're under the New Covenant and not the Old one). This of
course carries on into STAGE FOUR. Any time you spot an error
in your understructure you'll need to go back and fix it to
effectively move on. In fact, this is the very reason the Holy Spirit,
the "Spirit of Truth" (John 16:13), will reveal error to you, not so
you stubbornly go on your way naively believing that everything
taught you in STAGE TWO was exemplary and is never to be
questioned. Anyone who thinks like this will be stuck in STAGE
TWO the rest of their lives, at least to some degree.

Living and Dying in STAGE TWO

Speaking of which, numerous believers live and die in
STAGE TWO, sometimes because their pastors encourage it. In
other words, their elders groom the congregants to be dependent on
the organization. Why would they possibly do this? As noted
earlier, it's their way of "holding on" to their current fold by
intentionally keeping them in the dependent phase of STAGE
TWO.

Pastors who do this are usually STAGE TWO themselves, albeit at a higher level than their congregants. You might wonder how a pastor or any other fivefold minister could be STAGE TWO, but they're all over. Since these ministers are further along in STAGE TWO than their congregants they can certainly lead them, but because they themselves are primarily in STAGE TWO they *can't* lead their disciples into STAGE THREE or FOUR.

What characterizes pastors and other ministers who are mainly in STAGE TWO? They're typically "yes" men or women with a rigid sectarian spirit, regardless of the camp/sect, including Evangelical, Pentecostal and "non-denominational" ones. They may know the Bible, as far as their camp interprets it, and sometimes expertly so, but **1.** because they're not STAGE THREE they haven't learned to think outside of the box of their sect, and **2.** they don't know the Writer of the Word they preach, at least not in an actual relational sense. This doesn't mean they can't have an anointing to some degree—and by anointing I mean God's blessing and empowerment—but, if so, it's a limited STAGE TWO anointing and marred by the inherent errors of their camp/sect.

Nor does it mean that STAGE THREE and FOUR believers can't receive from ministers in STAGE TWO; that is, learn something from them. If you're humble and have a teachable spirit you can learn from any number of people. I once received revelation from a 12 year-old girl in a church, not to mention the LORD used a donkey to rebuke Balaam (Numbers 22:26-34). However, just because STAGE THREE or FOUR believers *can* learn from a minster in STAGE TWO, it doesn't mean they should hook up with their ministry and be subordinate to them. Such a scenario is a recipe for utter frustration simply because the STAGE THREE or FOUR believer is further along than the STAGE TWO minister. As such, the minister *can't* lead the believer. How can a minister at a lower spiritual level lead believers at a higher level? STAGE THREE or FOUR believers should hook up with ministries that have pastors and elders in STAGE FOUR. Remember this: Ministers can only take you as far as they are; they can't give what they don't have. This is an axiom.

Returning to the main point, believers live and die in STAGE TWO all the time. It's unfortunate, but it's just the way it is. And it's not always their pastor's fault. Some precious souls won't leave STAGE TWO even when pastors and elders do everything they can to inspire them to grow up spiritually. These believers simply don't want to move on to the increasing independence of STAGE THREE and the inherent risks thereof or, even more harrowing (to them), the Christ-led autonomy of STAGE FOUR. These higher stages represent the unknown and people are naturally wary of the unknown. So they just stay within the comforts and limitations of STAGE TWO. There isn't much you can do for them because they're staying in STAGE TWO **by their own choice**. We all have the God-given power of volition and we have to respect it, even when we know the person is making a mistake and limiting his or her life. Just love 'em, pray for 'em and continue to encourage them through the Word and leading of the Spirit. Amen.

Those Stuck in STAGE TWO Prefer the Rules Thereof

There are other reasons some believers choose to stay in STAGE TWO and essentially refuse to grow up spiritually. One reason is laziness. In some perverted sense it's easier to submit to an institution and the system of doctrines/rules thereof than to think for oneself (STAGE THREE). You'll see this mentality in Christians who wholly submit their lives to authoritarian churches that tell them precisely what to do and believe. As such, they don't have to think for themselves; they just follow the authoritarians and their commands or rules. The pastors of authoritarian churches, by the way, are almost always higher level STAGE TWO with their big heads entrenched in STAGE ONE in view of their arrogance.

Other reasons believers refuse to leave STAGE TWO are insecurity and fear. Some believers are so insecure that they need someone to tell them what to do and believe. They're simply not secure in who they are in Christ and, consequently, they're weak. As noted above, they're afraid of the responsibilities and freedoms that come with spiritual adulthood and therefore never really grow up. It's akin to the security of working for a company all your life rather than deal with the uncertainties of striking out on your own. Although the latter would provide a sense of adventure, freedom and change, the former provides security and comfort. Why risk the unknown? For this same reason millions of believers languish in STAGE TWO. They particularly "languish" if it's a dead fellowship.

Preferring the security of being an employee rather than being your own master is fine for the labor market, if that's what a person prefers, but it'll severely limit you in the realm of the spirit. It also makes you open prey for domineering non-ministers. There are plenty of authoritarians out there who are more than willing to take advantage of believers who refuse to take the reins of spiritual maturity. These could be legalists or libertines since legalism and libertinism are two sides of the same bad coin.

Since those who refuse to leave STAGE TWO don't have an intimate relationship with the LORD (STAGE FOUR) they have no choice but to divert to rules and regulations, meaning their faith is limited to focusing on outward obedience to the rules/doctrines of the institution rather than inward transformation through seeking and experiencing God on their own. This isn't to say they won't go through the motions of having a relationship, but this is chiefly for appearances sake. In some cases they may actually pray in their private time, but it's very rehearsed, one-sided and lifeless, like talking to a wall. They likely do this to convince themselves that they actually have a relationship with God. If your prayer time is dry, one-dimensional and boring, take note. It's not a good sign. True communion with the Fountain of Life should be an exciting, life-transforming experience (Psalm 36:9), not tedious and dull.

Those who experience the stirrings of STAGE THREE and FOUR, by contrast, will instinctively feel stifled by the constrictions of STAGE TWO. The box that God is put into by the institution will make them want to scream, and increasingly so. The eye-rolling unbiblical rules and well-intended, but stultifying supervision of STAGE TWO pastors and elders will begin to frustrate and even offend. These are growth pangs prompted by the Holy Spirit to inspire them to *leave* and move on to STAGE THREE and FOUR.

Non-Christian Substitutions

There are obvious secular substitutions to STAGE TWO. Prison is a good example. Individuals in the lower levels of STAGE ONE inevitably break the law because of their chaotic spiritual condition, which inevitably lands them in prison. Their new environment provides the parameters and order they need to escape the chaos of STAGE ONE, but as soon as they're released back into the public they revert back to STAGE ONE because they can't handle the freedom. They're *dependent* on the institution to keep them from iniquity, at least outwardly.

Religious and non-religious institutions are also substitutes, like Sciencefictionology, Mormonism, TM, rehabs, psyche wards, 12-step programs, martial arts programs and a gazillion others. They're not all bad, of course, and they do (try to) help the individual escape the darkness and chaos of STAGE ONE, but such disciplines all pale in comparison to the effectiveness of genuine Christianity (as opposed to sterile, religious "Christianity") because true Christianity solves humanity's root problem—the condition of spiritual death and the resulting separation from God.

The family can also be a substitute (and in the believer's life it plays an accessory role). For instance, individuals who grow up in strong families that have a wealth of love, order and discipline essentially grow up without experiencing the darkness and chaos of STAGE ONE. Such people are, in essence, *born* into STAGE TWO. This is normally a good thing and those with healthy families like this should be praising God that they largely skipped STAGE ONE. This only becomes a problem if the individual becomes arrogant (spoiled) by his or her good fortune, which is a sure slide into STAGE ONE, keeping in mind that arrogance—a superiority complex—is sin *numero uno* in God's eyes.

If we're talking about spiritually regenerated believers who grow up in godly families, they are indeed in STAGE TWO, but if we're talking about unbelievers who are unregenerated and therefore separate from God then, of course, they're not truly in STAGE TWO. They're only in STAGE TWO in the sense that their healthy family is acting as a substitution, providing the structure, rules, supervision and accountability that largely keeps them out of the darkness of STAGE ONE. However, they're still technically in STAGE ONE, albeit the higher levels. Because of their healthy family or other quality institution they have a foothold in STAGE TWO, but only in a substitutionary sense. Here's how it would look on the Four Stages diagram:

Unbelievers can also be in STAGE THREE and FOUR in a substitutionary sense. Through the structure provided by their substitutionary STAGE TWO they developed discipline and therefore eventually progress to substitutionary STAGE THREE where they function as free-thinking and responsible individuals. They can even reach substitutionary STAGE FOUR in that they experience glimmerings of God and truth.

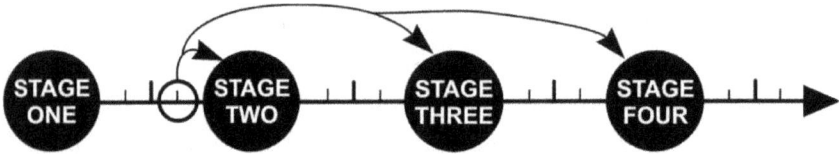

As you can see from the diagram, the unbeliever is squarely in STAGE ONE and can only experience the other stages in a vicarious sense.

Let me give you an example from my own life: I was a mixed-up unbeliever throughout my teen years and was therefore decidedly STAGE ONE, but I eventually learned discipline through various means (proxy STAGE TWO) and developed as a responsible individual to some degree by the time I was 18-19 (proxy STAGE THREE). Furthermore, throughout my teens I increasingly sought the truth and genuinely so. I wasn't born-again yet (John 3:3,6), but I had glimmerings of the LORD because I heard the gospel many times from different sources through those years and some Christians were interceding for me. This led to my salvation four months after my 20th birthday.

So there are non-Christian people who are spiritually un-regenerated, but they're experiencing STAGE TWO, THREE and FOUR in a substitutionary sense.

I said above that arrogance is sin *numero uno* in God's eyes. This brings up an important point...

STAGE FOUR Believers are *Humble*

STAGE FOUR believers are at the highest stage of spiritual growth, although not the highest *level,* as there are levels within each stage and STAGE FOUR is infinite since the capacity to know God is infinite. Because they're at the highest stage it's easy to assume they'd be arrogant, but this isn't the case at all. People who genuinely know God are extremely humble because (paraphrasing) "God resists the proud, but gives his favor to the humble" (James 4:6 & 1 Peter 5:5). As such, only the humble can get close to God.

If you know domineering Christians who love to bloviate, bluster and abuse, they're *not* in STAGE FOUR. They're in STAGE TWO or THREE with their big heads in STAGE ONE. A couple of ministers I met, for instance, had the tendency to "prove" their points through bluster or intimidation rather than what the Bible clearly and consistently teaches. When you come across these types you have to resist the temptation to stoop to their level. Ignore their covert (and sometimes overt) insults and intimidation and simply focus on the relevant biblical data. When they see that you won't submit to their manipulations they'll either **1.** get more insulting and abusive or **2.** end the discussion one way or another (if it's an email exchange, for example, they'll simply refuse to write back under the assumed guise that they're "too busy"). In cases of the former, continue to resist the temptation to respond in kind and focus on what the Word of God teaches in a balanced fashion, interpreting Scripture with Scripture. Only revert to tough love tactics if led of the Holy Spirit to do so, which Jesus did on occasion (e.g. Matthew 23:13-33). Whatever the case, you must not tolerate or condone this kind of pompous abuse—tactics of bluster and intimidation—even if the minister has an impressive ministry and decades of experience. If the individual is truly a great man or woman of God then s/he has no business behaving in this manner. If it's someone over you in the LORD you're still obligated to correct. Of course, you should correct in a respectful manner, particularly if the person is older than you, unless the situation calls for a more blunt approach.

I've known big-time ministers who have books, TV programs and world-reaching ministries who seem to have let it go to their head and are therefore rigid with the box into which they've put God (and themselves). If you happen to share a legitimate scriptural point that deviates from a dubious doctrine they've taught as gospel truth for decades they'll get irate and rashly insult you. Mature believers—that is, STAGE FOUR believers—don't get mad when someone merely disagrees with them; they humbly and honestly turn to God's Word and allow it to settle the matter in a thorough and balanced manner. In short, mature believers allow the Word of truth (John 17:17 & 2 Timothy 2:15) to reveal what's true and what's not true, including what's only partially true. This'll correct the other person. If he or she still disagrees then that's his/her problem.

I've noticed, unfortunately, that too many believers—including fivefold ministers—don't go by the authority of God's Word, but rather by the authority of religious tradition and the forefathers or foremothers of their camp. For instance, if you say something thoroughly biblical that disagrees with a religious slogan of their sect or what the founder teaches (or taught) they'll immediately put up a wall and the case will be closed. Why? Because they respect the word of a human authority above the Word of God. People like this, no matter how great their position, are still locked into STAGE TWO, even though they may have a foot or hand in the next two stages. It's frankly a puerile mindset.

Thankfully, I've known world-traveling ministers with impressive ministries who are incredibly humble. One minister I know, for instance, literally changed his last name to Servant. I met with him on a few occasions and his humility was palpable. I've met with other ministers whose ministries are 1/50th the size of his, but who were noticeably arrogant about their supposedly great position and accomplishments, the latter of which weren't very impressive. It's impossible for these types to relate to fellow believers as equals and they therefore tend to speak down to them or intimidate, even if it's subtle. I find it amusing whenever I see it, but not in a good way. They tend to posture and bloviate like they're great men or women of God when it's simply not the case. How do I know? Because, again, God actively opposes the proud but gives his favor to the humble. See for yourself:

> **"God opposes the proud but shows favor to the humble."**
>
> **James 4:6 & 1 Peter 5:5**

The passage is in quotes because James and Peter are paraphrasing Proverbs 3:34. Consequently, the verse appears no less than *three times in God's Word*—once in the Old Testament and twice in the New Testament. Do ya think the LORD's trying to tell us something? He's driving home that He *resists* the arrogant—*opposes* them—but extends favor and honor to the humble. If God resists and opposes the proud—including those who say they're Christians and even function in the ministry—then he's obviously not close to them, right? And if God's not close to the person they're obviously not in STAGE FOUR because STAGE FOUR is the stage where believers know and walk humbly before God.

STAGE FOUR Believers have an Equalitarian Attitude

I said above that it's impossible for those infected with arrogance to relate to others as equals and, as such, they tend to be condescending and intimidating. Anyone who wants to be great in the kingdom of God (STAGE FOUR) *cannot* have these traits active in their lives. Notice what Jesus said on the matter:

"they [Pharisees and teachers of the law]
**love to be greeted with respect in the
marketplaces and to be called 'Rabbi' by others.**

**(8) "But you are not to be called 'Rabbi,'
for you have one Teacher, and <u>you are all
brothers</u>. (9) And do not call anyone on earth
'father,' for you have one Father, and he is in
heaven. (10) Nor are you to be called instructors,
for you have one Instructor, the Messiah. (11)
<u>The greatest among you will be your servant.</u>
(12) For <u>those who exalt themselves will be
humbled</u>, and those who humble themselves will
be exalted."**

Matthew 23:7-11

The legalistic religious leaders of Israel relished being referred to with an honorary title like "Rabbi," which means 'teacher' (John 1:38). Jesus said that's not the way it's supposed to be in the church because we "are all brothers," which indicates the equalitarian nature of leadership in the body of Christ. No matter who the pastor or teacher or prophet or apostle or evangelist is, we "are all brothers (and sisters)" in Christ Jesus.

Whenever you sense ministers trying to impress upon you the great gulf between you and them—as if you're lowly and they're great—it's not a good sign. I've experienced this a few times and it's always a turn-off, to say the least. I could see if I was newly saved or even within the first decade of my Christian walk, but these occasions happened after I was 15 years in the Lord. One time I was out to coffee with a minister and he decided to pray over me because I had just accomplished something (I can't even remember what it was) and so he clasped my hands and prayed, "Father God, I thank you for my brother Dirk; I now consider him an equal." While this might not sound too bad on paper it smacked of arrogance in real life—like we weren't equals before the occasion. I told my wife about it and she just rolled her eyes. On another occasion I took a pastor for a hike and went to coffee afterward where he complained about people in the church whom he felt were getting too chummy. He told me, "I'm their pastor not their buddy!" Of course he was indirectly saying this to me since we had just taken a hike together and were having coffee.

In the body of Christ the lines between overseers and other believers should be soft. Those in the fivefold ministry (Ephesians 4:11-14) are *servants* to the rest, not vice versa. In fact, the very word 'minister' *means* "servant."

Furthermore, Jesus said "those who exalt themselves will be humbled and those who humble themselves will be exalted" (verse 12).

The "Title Syndrome"

Do you see ministers obsessed with honorary titles, like "Pastor," "Reverend," "Apostle," "Doctor," "Master Prophet" and so on? (Please notice I said obsessed). It's not a good sign in light of what Jesus taught. This was the way religious leaders were during Christ's earthly ministry and you'll unfortunately see the same thing today. Of course, **hard-working servant-leaders are to be respected** (1 Thessalonians 5:12) and Ephesians 4:11 shows that there are legitimate leadership gifts in the body of Christ— apostles, prophets, evangelists, pastors and teachers—but these are gifts, anointings or positions, *not* titles. If you disagree, try to find *one* occurrence in the New Testament where a leader is addressed as Pastor So-and-So, Apostle So-and-So or Reverend So-and-So. You won't find it because it's an unbiblical practice. Paul was simply called "Paul" and other significant leaders were also referred to by name, like Peter, Apollos, Timothy and Barnabas (e.g. 2 Peter 3:15, Galatians 2:6-9).[4] The Holy Spirit inspired these passages through men of God (2 Peter 1:20-21) and the Bible is the blueprint for authentic Christianity. In other words, **this is the example God's Word sets for believers throughout the Church Age**. If these great men of God could be referred to simply by their first names how much more so men and women of God today, great or small?

Let me stress that I'm not saying every leader in the body of Christ who utilizes a title is a wicked counterfeit frothing at the mouth with arrogance. I'm just saying that titles for servant-leaders is not a biblical practice and therefore those who are obsessed with titles have a problem because there's no biblical basis for the practice, except that the Pharisees and teachers of the law relished honorary titles. What *godly* man or woman wants to be associated with such religious cons?

Jesus said that the greatest amongst us—meaning those in STAGE FOUR—should have servant's hearts and not be pompous authoritarians who revel in the power and honor of their position (Matthew 23:11). Paul taught the same thing (2 Corinthians 4:5). Let me hastily add, however, that **having a humble servant's heart and an equalitarian attitude doesn't mean being a wimpy, powerless milksop.** Anyone close to the Almighty will be anything but because God is the awesome Fountain of Life who gushes life and power into the hearts of anyone who gets close to Him (Psalm 36:9), which is why we see dynamic men and women of God throughout the Old and New Testaments doing all kinds of bold and amazing things with God's blessing and empowerment.

---

[4] Yes, John referred to himself as "the elder" (2 John & 3 John 1:1), but that's simply because he was an elder in the church who happened to be quite aged (close to 90 when he wrote these two brief epistles), not to mention he walked with Christ. In short, "the elder" was his nickname and not an honorary title; if church leaders were intent on giving him a highfalutin title it certainly wouldn't be as generic as "the elder." Also, Paul referred to himself as the spiritual "father" of the Corinthian believers, but that's only because he pioneered that fellowship; he never used "father" as a title, as in "Father Paul."

Furthermore, Godly men and women aren't nicey-wicey doormats. Sometimes walking in love calls for *tough* love and sometimes the kindest thing you can do for a person is to boldly tell them the awful truth. Jesus did this when he powerfully cleansed the temple of greedy charlatans and carnal riff-raff whereupon he instilled fear in the religious leaders and amazement in the onlookers (Mark 11:15-18); Paul did it when he radically rebuked Elymas the sorcerer for trying to keep the proconsul of Cyprus from the faith (Acts 13:8-12); and Peter did it with another sorcerer in Samaria (Acts 8:9-24).

Simply put, insisting on a title (not a job position, a title) smacks of insecurity. The problem with this is that strong men and women of God are not insecure. They're genuinely close to the LORD and therefore are perfectly secure with who they are, whom they serve and what their God-given mission is.

Beyond pride and insecurity, the reason some fivefold ministers—mostly pastors—insist on a title is to subconsciously drill into the heads of their congregants (and others) that they're the authority of the assembly in question. While this seems legitimate and harmless on the surface there's an obvious drawback: It unconsciously promotes the sheeple mentality of STAGE TWO where believers are *dependent* upon their pastors. In short, it promotes spiritual immaturity in the long run.

If you're a fivefold minister, here's a test to see if you have a problem with the "title syndrome": If you're even a little disappointed or, worse, offended when someone fails to address you with a title like "Pastor John" you have a problem and need to change for the positive, i.e. REPENT.

Mentor and Mentee Dynamics

So in discussing Christian leadership Jesus emphasized how believers "are all brothers (and sisters)" and how the person who wants to be first must become last and so on (Matthew 23:7-

11 & Mark 9:35). Although such instructions don't mean Christian leaders should be spineless doormats it certainly conveys a humble and equalitarian attitude amongst the brethren and sistren that should increase as we advance in the faith (and, yes, "sistren" is an actual word).

With this in mind, I'd like to make a few observations about spiritual mentors and protégés. Paul and Timothy are a good example of a mentor/mentee relationship in the New Testament. In such relationships should the protégé concede to the perspective of the mentor even if the mentor is wrong? What is the basis for spiritual truth in the body of Christ? God's Word. If the mentee clearly discerns that the mentor is in error should the mentee speak up, particularly if the mentor is trying to "prove" his/her point on mere bluster rather than thorough scriptural evidence? Of course the protégé should speak up, keeping in view that there's a right way and a wrong way to disagree with someone who's over you in the Lord or, at least, older than you. Out of respect for the mentor you'll want to leave room for him or her to keep their dignity because, after all, they are the mentor.

However, what if the mentor refuses to receive the correction simply because he or she is the mentor? If this happens it's an indication of the infection of arrogance—a superiority complex—which isn't a good sign. In such occasions you have no choice but to make a stand with the truth and let the chips fall where they may. If the mentor severs ties with you then shame on him or her.

Sometimes the lines between mentor and mentee are blurred for various reasons. Say, for instance, you read a book, article or blog by a certain minister and proceed to learn many things from him or her, which means that the minister automatically becomes your mentor since you are learning from him/her (keeping in mind that protégé means "pupil"). Does this make the minister the ultimate authority on every spiritual topic? Does it mean that you can't legitimately disagree with him or her if it's clear he/she is wrong in one area or another? Of course not. Jesus Christ is the "Chief Shepherd" and fivefold ministers are simply under shepherds (1 Peter 5:1-4).

Bear in mind that **spiritually mature** mentors—i.e. STAGE FOUR—won't be threatened by the questions of a mentee. And disagreements won't aggravate them as long as they can be scripturally proven. In fact, **true mentors *want* their pupils to exceed them and therefore they *welcome* questions and contentions as the mentee grows.** Mentors who get irate when mentees merely question them or disagree based on the Scriptures show they're not spiritually mature, meaning they're not STAGE FOUR.

For anyone who would argue that a protégé *couldn't* possibly reach a point where he/she knows more than the mentor in one area or another, this is frankly silly and unrealistic. After all, David proclaimed he had greater insights and understanding than *his* teachers and elders (Psalm 119:99-100). Why do you think God recorded this in His Word? Because *this will happen* whenever a person has the same heart of David, meaning "a man (or woman) after God's own heart."

Needless to say, mentors who resort to bluster, intimidation or insults in scriptural discussions disqualify themselves as mentors and show that they're not worthy of your respect (unless they humbly repent, of course). They're spiritually immature and infected by arrogance. *Leave them* (Matthew 15:14).

Lastly, there's only one flawless teacher during the Church Age and that's the Holy Spirit (John 16:7-13). Men and women of God—no matter how knowledgeable, gifted and spiritually mature—are human beings and therefore imperfect. They're not infallible or perfect in knowledge and therefore don't know it all. They have weaknesses and will inevitably let you down. That's why you'll move away from dependency on human mentors as you advance in the Lord. You'll instead lean more and more on the Holy Spirit; and the Holy Spirit is God. Believers who are dependent upon human mentors are not spiritually mature. They're in STAGE TWO or, at best, STAGE THREE. Please notice I said "dependent upon human mentors," which is different than *receiving from* them. Those in STAGE FOUR are humble and wise enough to always seek out and receive from other people in their area of expertise and wisdom—in fact, they're enthusiastic about it because they're *learners* who are constantly learning. So receiving from people's area of strength is always good, but this is different than being perpetually dependent on them, which isn't good.

We'll look at the importance of cultivating the attitude of a learner in Chapter Five.

Pastors are Shepherds Looking for Sheep to Shepherd

There's something everyone should know about pastors. The Greek word for 'pastor' is *poimén (poy-MAYN)*, which literally means "shepherd" and figuratively "a person the Lord raises up to *care for* the well-being of His flock." This is the call of all genuine pastors and so they're naturally on the lookout for sheep that *need* shepherding. The less shepherding a believer needs—i.e. care, feeding and supervision—the less interested the pastor will be in him or her. The exception would be mature believers who can assist the pastor in shepherding the sheep; that is, subordinate pastors. If you don't qualify for either of these the pastor in question won't likely be very interested in you. There's nothing wrong with this because it's just the way it is.

I point this out for those who have grown beyond STAGE TWO and are well into STAGE THREE or the early levels of STAGE FOUR. Unless you're called to a subordinate pastoral position in a fellowship—including elder, counselor or supporter—the pastor simply won't be interested in you. Don't be offended in these cases because the pastor *shouldn't* be interested in you. You don't need the pastor and pastors are only interested in people who need their services. The ultimate purpose of pastors is to shepherd believers to the point where they no longer need the shepherding of a pastor.

I was well into STAGE THREE and the early levels of STAGE FOUR when I noticed that pastors at churches weren't very interested in me as I was looking for a local fellowship. I should say "we" because my wife was with me, but I want to keep this on a personal level. They'd essentially eye me up and down to discern where I was at spiritually. When they discerned that I didn't need them to walk closely with the LORD they didn't want much to do with me. Instead of becoming offended and badmouthing them—immature signs of STAGE ONE or TWO—I prayed for them and continued to seek the Lord's will for my life, which ultimately led to the birth of Fountain of Life Teaching Ministry and all that goes with it.

I encourage you to do the same if you experience this in your walk. Don't revile pastors for being what they are—pastors. Instead, praise God that you no longer need them and are free to move on to new levels in the spirit. If you're going to be mad at anyone be mad at yourself for trying to stay in the childhood or youth stage of Christianity when you've outgrown both.

By the way, this is not to say that believers can't be blessed by the ministries of pastors who don't want them in their fellowships. You can receive from anyone who rightly divides and serves God's Word. Eat the meat and spit out the bones or, as the Bible puts it: "Test everything. Hold on to the good" (1 Thessalonians 5:21).

Rigid Sectarianism—"Factions"—is of the Flesh

Earlier we talked about how those who get stuck in STAGE TWO inevitably develop a spirit of staunch sectarianism whereupon they increasingly view "outsiders" with an eye of suspicion. By 'outsider' I mean anyone who's not part of their church/sect or anyone who has chosen to leave. Consider this scriptural example:

> **"Master," said John, "we saw a man driving out demons in your name and we tried to stop him, <u>because he is not one of us</u>."**
> **(50) "Do not stop him," Jesus said, "for whoever is not against you is for you."**
> **Luke 9:49-50**

As you can see, John and the other disciples were upset that someone besides them was driving out demons in Jesus' name and their knee-jerk response was to oppose him. This is the spirit of rigid sectarianism. Those who cop such an attitude view people outside their group with a suspicious, rivalrous eye. What's absurd is that this man was doing an incredibly good work—driving out demons—but it didn't matter to John and the other disciples because they were blinded by their sectarian spirit.

Jesus put an immediate stop to this nonsense. His response was simple: "Do not stop him, for whoever is not against you is for you." Obviously it didn't bother the Lord that the man was operating outside their group. It didn't irk him in the least that he didn't go to Jesus' "seminary." The man was doing a good work and he was obviously on their side, so what was the problem? There wasn't one, but those infected by rigid sectarianism will always create a problem when it concerns someone outside the comforts of the box with which they've put themselves and God.

The Messiah didn't come down too hard on his disciples here. He saw that they were developing a sectarian spirit and simply nipped it in the bud. Jesus' general strategy on such occasions was to correct the negative behavior or attitude in a fairly mild manner and only take a sterner approach when the person or persons failed to respond positively. This should be our approach as well.

The reason Jesus corrected them was because staunch sectarianism is of the flesh, which is why Paul listed it as one of the works of the flesh:

> **The acts of the flesh are obvious: sexual immorality, impurity and debauchery; (20) idolatry and witchcraft; hatred, discord, jealousy, fits of rage, selfish ambition, dissensions, <u>factions</u> (21) and envy; drunkenness, orgies, and the like. I warn you, as I did before, that those who live like this will not inherit the kingdom of God.**
>
> **Galatians 5:19-21**

The word 'factions' in the Greek is *hairesis (HAH-ee-res-is)*, meaning "a religious or philosophical sect." There's nothing wrong with being part of a sect, of course, as long as it's healthy and legitimate. In fact, to go through STAGE TWO it's nigh *necessary* to hook up with a specific group; and every group has its governing structure and a list of official doctrines, written or unwritten. To function in this organization believers *have* to submit to the corresponding servant-leaders and assent to their major doctrines, which doesn't mean they'll agree 100% because those in STAGE TWO simply don't know enough to agree with absolute certainty. So there's nothing wrong with being a part of a sect in this manner. It's *sectarianism* that's of the flesh; and, more specifically, rigid sectarianism. This is what 'factions' refers to in the above passage.

Believers make a mistake when they join a church/camp/sect and then limit themselves to the official ministers and doctrines therein. By doing so they cut themselves off from any minister or teaching that doesn't jibe with their group. Why is this a mistake? Because it will bar them from vital biblical information that can bless them and set them free in one area or another. A good example would be the baptism of the Holy Spirit. If you're part of a group that staunchly insists that the gift of glossolalia passed away when the last of the original apostles died circa 100 AD then it's likely you'll never experience this awesome gift as long as you're a loyal follower of said group. I could list scores of other examples off the top of my head. For example, if you join a camp that supports amillennialism and strictly embrace their theology you can pretty much kiss goodbye the awesome biblical truths that reveal the nature of eternal life and everything surrounding it—literal glorified bodies, the new Jerusalem, the new earth, the new heavens (universe), etc.[5]

When I first became a Christian I went to a few churches for a couple of years before finally settling down in a quality fellowship for a decade where I was fed the best spiritual diet you could imagine. Like most people in the beginning levels of STAGE TWO I thought this church and its camp was the best on earth and in some ways it was; it was a top-of-the-line ministry. However, I didn't make the mistake of only feeding from the teachings of this ministry/sect. At least half my spiritual diet was from my own studies in the Scriptures, which I supplemented with the teachings from quality ministers inside and outside this camp via books, tapes, radio programs and so on.

---

[5] For insights on the nature of eternal life, see the corresponding teaching at the Fountain of Life website, also available in the Epilogue of *Sheol Know*.

Somehow I instinctively knew that it was a mistake to limit myself to *one* general mindset in the body of Christ and I've been exponentially blessed because of it.

Sectarians would argue that doing this creates confusion in believers because they'll expose themselves to conflicting beliefs. For instance, one camp will say that Jehovah is a healing God and it's *always* His will to heal whereas another group will argue that the LORD sometimes heals, but it's not always his will and so you can never be sure. Yes, facing such contradictions can cause immature believers to throw the baby out with the bathwater, so to speak, and use it as an excuse to backtrack to STAGE ONE. Keep in mind, however, that people like this would've likely found some other excuse to revert back to STAGE ONE. Let 'em go. Jesus said it's only those who "continue in his word" and don't give up who find the truth and are set free (John 8:31-32). God is a rewarder of those who diligently seek Him, not of those who throw in the towel because one ministry teaches one thing and another contradicts it and it frustrates them (Hebrews 11:6).

Rigid Sectarianism is Spiritual Immaturity

When Jesus' disciples automatically condemned someone outside their group who was simply doing a good work they revealed their immaturity. They were STAGE TWO believers at this point. Jesus, on the other hand, was spiritually mature—STAGE FOUR—and that's why he didn't mind one bit that this guy was driving out demons in His name. In fact, Jesus was no doubt elated that someone believed strongly enough to take the initiative and advance God's kingdom in such an authoritative manner—and the man didn't even have formal backing!

I see unhealthy sectarianism fairly regularly in the church and it always repels me. Here's a good example: I worked with a guy for a number of years and, at first, he couldn't say enough praise about the church he was attending. This is good to a degree.

We *should* have a positive attitude toward the fellowship God calls us to; otherwise we should go somewhere else. Yet this guy's attitude bordered on excessive. He kept trying to get me to come to his church for this or that function when I was perfectly happy at the fellowship I was serving. Then something went sour and he left his church. All his accolades suddenly vanished. Although he didn't revert to overt backbiting, he now had *nothing* good to say about his former assembly. A year or so later he found another fellowship and, once again, it was the greatest church on earth and any person who wasn't going there was somehow a lesser Christian and he looked down on them. Not openly, of course, it was just the general vibe he gave. Frankly, this is arrogance—a superiority complex—which isn't a good trait to develop because "God **opposes** the proud, but gives his grace to the humble" (James 4:6 & 1 Peter 5:5). A few years later he left that church. Apparently it wasn't so great after all, huh?

I ran into this same guy recently and happened to mention a minister who functioned outside of the normal Christian circuit. Hostility suddenly flared on his face and it was clear that he couldn't stand the man. Did this minister offend him in some personal way? Nope. He rejected him simply because the minister operated outside the typical church circles with which he was familiar. God forbid that the Lord would use someone outside conventional church circuits to serve people most believers would never likely reach!

Anytime you see professing Christians showing signs of staunch sectarianism like this, it signifies spiritual immaturity. It doesn't matter if they're elders, pastors, deacons, worship leaders or 80 years old. It's a one-dimensional, puerile mindset. It's spiritual tunnel vision. Yes, we all go through a period in our formative years thinking our church or camp is the best and most blessed on the planet—it's the mentality of someone in the lower-to-mid levels of STAGE TWO—but then we hopefully grow up. Unfortunately, all believers grow older, but not all believers grow up. And that's why this book exists—to inspire people to progress to spiritual maturity!

Believers in STAGE TWO Argue Doctrine from a Sectarian Standpoint

You may have noticed that certain believers defend or denounce certain doctrines based on sectarian loyalties and boundaries. For instance, someone might denounce something you believe or teach because there's a group he/she objects to that also teaches it, at least in some form. Or say you teach something that doesn't gel with the religious tradition of another believer and s/he instantly writes it off as false doctrine. Let me give you an example: In my book *Hell Know* I have a fairly long section on the Judgment Seat of Christ. A minister wrote me and lambasted me for deviating from Evangelical tradition. As I read his email it became clear that he didn't even read the section of the book in question, at least not fully. Moreover his scriptural "evidence" was scant and he relied on quoting Evangelical slogans that aren't actually in the Bible. I wrote him back the same day and explained in detail. The only answer I got back was chirping crickets.

Here's a truth that all spiritually mature believers embrace: It doesn't matter what one group believes or another group believes on any issue; the only thing that matters is what the truth is. Why? Because truth literally means "reality." Truth simply means the way it really is. My point is that the truth is the truth regardless of what any person or group believes. So when you're trying to discover the truth on a certain issue it's irrelevant what this or that sect believes. All that matters is the truth and the truth is the clear revelation of the Word of God (John 17:17) as we continue in it, interpreting in context and in light of the greater context of the entire Bible (John 8:31-32). Here are the four common-sense rules of hermeneutics; that is, Bible interpretation:

1. **Context is king:** Meaning the surrounding text reveals the obvious meaning of each passage

2. **Scripture interprets Scripture:** Meaning every passage must be interpreted in light of the context of the entire Bible and that the Bible itself is its best interpreter. In other words, one's interpretation of a passage must gel with what the rest of Scripture teaches; the more overt and detailed passages obviously expand our understanding of the more sketchy and ambiguous ones.

3. **Take the Bible literally unless it's clear that figurative language is being used:** In which case you look for the literal truth that the symbolism intends to convey.

4. **If the plain sense makes sense—and is in harmony with the rest of Scripture—don't look for any other sense lest you end up with nonsense:** This includes the "plain sense" of the whole of Scripture on any given topic. In other words, if an individual or group comes up with an interpretation that is opposed to the plain-sense meaning that all the passages in the Bible obviously point to on that subject then it must be rejected. This fourth rule is essentially the other three combined.

These "rules" are really just common-sense guidelines for discovering truth and being set free from religious error. Although the Bible is simple enough that the simplest of persons can receive from it and be blessed, it's also deep and complex, which means that as believers grow in the Lord they naturally grow in knowledge, understanding and wisdom. As such, one believer might have a grasp on a passage or topic and another might have a fuller understanding. A good example of this can be seen in Acts 18:24-26 where Apollos, a very learned man and powerful speaker, had a limited understanding of the gospel of Jesus Christ. What he knew was good and accurate, as far as he understood it, but it wasn't a full or complete understanding. Aquila and Pricilla discerned this when they heard him speak; so they took Apollos aside, and "explained to him the way of God more adequately" (verse 26).

Staunch sectarians aren't like this, however; they argue for or against a doctrine based purely on sectarianism. If what you teach doesn't gel with their sect you're automatically wrong; if what you teach is adhered to by a group they object to you're wrong. What the Scriptures clearly and consistently teach on the topic is irrelevant to them. It's a spiritually immature mindset and decidedly STAGE TWO.

What about Godly People who are Rigidly Sectarian?

I said earlier that there's nothing wrong with being part of a sect, as long as it's healthy and legitimate, which means there's also nothing wrong with being a fivefold minister within a sect. In fact, it's easier to minister and pioneer churches within an existing camp than to pioneer as a non-sectarian from scratch for obvious reasons.

However, the more spiritually mature a believer is the less sectarian he or she will be. Truly godly believers see the body of Christ with an increasingly universal eye rather than the limited lens of their relatively small group. You'll come across such believers and ministers in every legitimate camp. They're sectarian because they belong to a group and operate within its boundaries, but they're not rigidly sectarian. There's nothing wrong with this and these believers are godly and mature, i.e. STAGE FOUR.

Unfortunately, there are some believers in ministry who are staunchly sectarian and they're definitely not STAGE FOUR. They're not even STAGE THREE. How do I know? Because to be STAGE THREE you have to be able to think and function independently of your sect/church and these people are unable to do this, which is why they're so staunch about their sect. Even if someone who's rigidly sectarian shows signs of genuine godliness—i.e. spiritual maturity—they're still manacled to STAGE TWO. It may be high level STAGE TWO, but it's STAGE TWO nevertheless. Such believers clearly have a hand or finger in the next two stages, but because of their blatant faction-ism they're decidedly STAGE TWO and therefore still spiritually immature to some degree. Here's how such a person would appear on the Four Stages diagram:

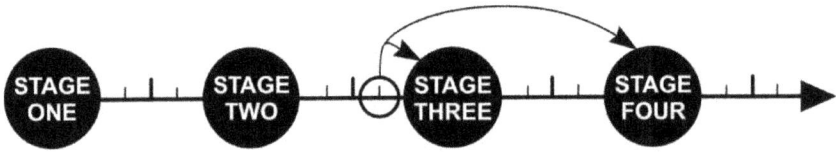

Understanding the "Communal Spirit"— Good and Bad

There's a mindset that develops amongst the members of any group, which I call a communal spirit. Every organized group of people develops such a "spirit," including marriages, families, clubs, companies, cities and nations. It's the general social mindset of the people within the community in question and it can be good or bad or somewhere in between.

Church fellowships develop a communal spirit. Take, for instance, the seven churches of Asia Minor that Jesus evaluated in Revelation 2-3. Generally speaking, the Lord accessed these assemblies collectively and not as individuals, which shows that His descriptions were in reference to a communal spirit and not an individual one. The church in Philadelphia, for instance, was known for faithfulness and perseverance whereas the church in Laodicea was known for being lukewarm. Most of the other churches were known for both good and bad traits, like the Ephesians who were acknowledged for their good deeds, hard work and perseverance, but were corrected for losing their passion for the LORD on a relational level.

In the 1800s a white man was assimilated into a Native tribe for years, but later re-assimilated with his own people. He chronicled his experiences in a book where he described the communal spirit that he encountered in the tribe. I forget the name of the book, but he wrote of his experience in terms of being in a "fog." When he eventually returned to American civilization he felt as if he had "woken up."

The congregants of a fellowship whose pastor and staff are in STAGE TWO will experience a religious fog. This "fog" will likely increase the longer they stay at the fellowship and, consequently, the longer they stay the more difficult it will be to break free of it.

There was a big church in my area in the late 80s where the pastor had an overtly authoritarian spirit. I know because I heard quite a few of his sermons on radio and cassette. He had an overwhelming air and it was easy to see why people would follow him, but I didn't sense any love or joy in his words. I developed a friendship with someone who attended this church for a season. Some of his relatives and friends were members, but they were so wowed by the pastor's natural leadership qualities that they failed to see his potentially harmful spirit. My friend, on the other hand, wasn't so wowed. He said he visited the church many times before deciding not to stay. He told his relatives and friends, "He's a charismatic speaker and all, but I just don't see any love or joy there." It wasn't much later that the church had two mass exoduses over a period of about a year.[6] By this point the church had a bad reputation in the community and it never really recovered. The pastor died prematurely a dozen years later.

---

[6] Not splits, since a split is when those who leave a church start their own church. An exodus is when believers leave and disperse to other fellowships.

Before the breakdown and decline of this church there were red flags of authoritarianism everywhere: congregants had to get the pastor's approval for large purchases, like a refrigerator; if someone left the church his or her relatives and friends were instructed to cut all ties; people were encouraged to quit their well-paying jobs and start their own businesses; men with longer hair were pressured to cut it and maintain shorter hair length; the entrance gates were closed and the doors locked during services; believers were discouraged from going to the restroom during the ridiculously long Sunday services; various individuals were literally screamed at in front of the congregation if the pastor thought they were going astray; etc. If you ever saw the excellent 1980 film *Guyana Tragedy: The Story of Jim Jones*, this church was verging on being that authoritarian.

Since the Bible plainly teaches that pastors are not to "lord it over" believers (1 Peter 5:1-4), they have no business telling congregants where to work, how to wear their hair, what kind of car to buy, what kind of clothes to wear, what style of music to listen to, what kind of movies to watch, etc. They're not the final authority in believers' lives, God is. Believers should simply be fed the Word of God and encouraged to develop a relationship with the Lord. This includes teaching them important principles, like how to guard their hearts as the wellspring of life (Proverbs 4:23). As they grow they'll naturally make their own decisions about these types of things.

At any rate, before the decline of this church it had a communal spirit of arrogance. Why? Because the congregants took on the spirit of their authoritarian pastor. Waitresses at local restaurants would dread the groups of congregants that would come to eat after services because they behaved with a palpable air of pomposity.

My wife and I were part of a fellowship for about seven years. The church had numerous positive elements and I was ultimately accepted as a regular teacher, giving sermons roughly every other week. The longer we stayed, however, the more negatives we observed. For instance, there was toleration of a relative of the pastor who was a pathological liar and ran around the church slandering people, including elders, which naturally created strife and caused quality people to leave from time to time.

I call this the "Eli Syndrome" based on the biblical account of the priest of Shiloh, Eli, and his tolerance of his wicked sons. This is off-topic a bit, but it ties into the main point: Eli's two sons were "in the ministry" but are described in the Bible as wicked men who had no regard for the LORD and even fornicated with the young women who served at the tabernacle (1 Samuel 2:12,17,22)! Although Eli rebuked his sons at one point it's clear that his heart wasn't in it, so to speak, and his sons continued in their wicked ways (verses 23-25). What was going on? Eli loved his sons, as any parent, but he foolishly only loved them with soft, feminine love. This was a huge mistake and ultimately resulted in God's judgment, which entailed the premature death of both sons, as well as the capture of the Ark of the Covenant, Eli's own death, the death of his daughter-in-law and the departure of God's anointing from his direct bloodline (1 Samuel 4:11,18-22). This could have all been avoided if only Eli would've been willing to love his sons with the necessary tough love, which would involve more than just a half-hearted verbal correction. It would mean a stern public rebuke and removal from the ministry altogether until they humbly repented and proved themselves. Loving his sons solely with gentle love resulted in their deaths whereas implementing tough love would have saved them. Are you getting this? Tough love would have literally saved their lives, not to mention Eli's ministry. It goes without saying that tough love is sometimes necessary. It's a good thing, not bad.[7]

---

[7] See the teaching "Gentle Love and Tough Love" at the Fountain of Life website for more details on this topic.

You'll occasionally see evidence of this "Eli Syndrome" in today's churches. A pastor will grant status to some undeserving kin, usually children, grandchildren or siblings, which doesn't necessarily have to be an official position. The pastor will then tend to condone the relatives' carnal antics, making excuses for them, etc. As long as you get along with these relatives you'll have the pastor's favor, but if you dare take a stand against any carnality you'll be blacklisted in one way or another and eventually forced to leave. Like Eli, the pastor may offer a weak verbal correction for appearances sake while the relatives continue to wreak havoc, overtly or covertly. There's only one sad end to the Eli Syndrome: The corruption of the ministry as sin works like yeast through the dough of the fellowship and the inevitable departure of God's presence and anointing. If only the pastor would implement tough love!

This is what was going on at the church Carol & I were attending. There were times when I instinctively had to take a break from attending services and I didn't know why; I just knew I had to take a break and keep my head clear. Of course churches with a STAGE TWO mentality don't take too kindly to those who take breaks from services, especially if you're a teacher, and so the carnal tongues started wagging. Nevertheless, when I needed to take a break I took a break and I didn't ask for the pastor's permission. This had nothing to do with rebellion, but the simple fact that I needed to rest and get refreshed (I was working a full-time secular job at the time). Whether the pastor approved or not, I had to do what I had to do to stay healthy.

It wasn't until a few years after leaving this assembly that I understood why I had to occasionally take breaks and refresh. *I was instinctively preventing myself from getting sucked into the negative communal spirit of this fellowship.* I was wisely keeping the religious fog of that assembly at bay—preventing it from getting its claws stuck in me. Consequently, when the LORD called us to leave after seven years it wasn't difficult to depart because I never let its negative communal spirit get its clutches in me. If you're at a fellowship and experience such a religious fog you'll have to be careful to keep yourself from getting sucked into it. Seek the Lord about whether or not you should stay and certainly leave if (or when) He gives you the go-ahead.

Thankfully, churches can have a good communal spirit, like the aforementioned church in Philadelphia, as well as the church in Smyrna (Revelation 3:7-13 & 2:8-11). The church that I went to for a decade from 1986-1996 when I was in STAGE TWO had a quality communal spirit. It wasn't a perfect assembly—no fellowship is—but it had a healthy communal spirit and I was exponentially blessed. Ideally you'll want to hook up with a ministry that has a healthy collective character, particularly if you're in STAGE TWO. The exception would be if you're spiritually mature—i.e. STAGE FOUR—and the Lord's calling you to serve at a church and help set them free from a negative communal spirit. Chapter 9 of my book *Legalism Unmasked* shows how to do this.

Chapter Four

Darkness, Childhood, Youth & Maturity

In <u>Chapter One</u> we saw that John referred to all Four Stages of Spiritual Growth in this passage:

> **Anyone who claims to be in the light but hates a brother or sister is still <u>in the darkness</u>. (10) Anyone who loves their brother and sister lives in the light, and there is nothing in them to make them stumble. (11) But anyone who hates a brother or sister is <u>in the darkness</u> and walks around <u>in the darkness</u>. They do not know where they are going, because the darkness has blinded them.**

(12) I am writing to you, dear <u>children</u>, because your sins have been forgiven on account of his name.

(13) I am writing to you, <u>fathers</u>, because you know him who is from the beginning.

I am writing to you, <u>young men</u>, because you have overcome the evil one.

(14) I write to you, dear <u>children</u>, because you know the Father.

I write to you, <u>fathers</u>, because you know him who is from the beginning.

I write to you, <u>young men</u>, because you are strong, and the word of God lives in you, and you have overcome the evil one.

1 John 2:9-14

The phrase "in the darkness" in verses 9-11 refers to the condition of spiritual death where people are dead to God and therefore "in the darkness." This is a reference to STAGE ONE.

Verses 12-14 refer to the three stages a person goes through once they're "made alive with Christ" (Ephesians 2:5 & Colossians 2:13). "Children" refers to STAGE TWO, "young men" to STAGE THREE and "fathers" to STAGE FOUR. Since there's neither male nor female in Christ (Galatians 3:28) we can broaden these terms as such: children, young people and parents or, better yet, **childhood**, **youth** and **maturity**. Let's fit these into our Four Stages diagram:

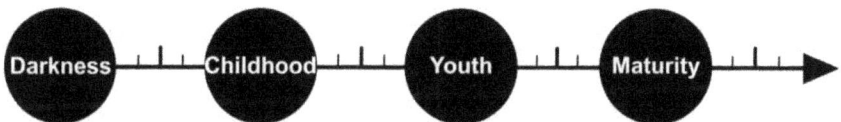

Now we'll consider John's distinctions of each of the Four Stages of Spiritual Growth:

STAGE ONE: "In the Darkness"

Notice again how the Holy Spirit through John describes being in STAGE ONE:

> **Anyone who claims to be in the light but hates a brother or sister is still in the darkness. (10) Anyone who loves their brother and sister lives in the light, and there is nothing in them to make them stumble. (11) But anyone who hates a brother or sister is in the darkness and walks around in the darkness. They do not know where they are going, because the darkness has blinded them.**
>
> **1 John 2:9-11**

We can derive four things from this description. Those in STAGE ONE:

1. are in the darkness.
2. are inclined toward hatred to some degree (which doesn't necessarily mean *all* people in STAGE ONE are inclined to hatred).
3. do not know where they're going beyond temporal ambitions.
4. are blinded in a spiritual sense.

People in STAGE ONE are in the darkness whether they know it or not. While those at the higher levels of STAGE ONE can be very moral due to substitutionary forms of STAGE TWO they're still in the darkness because they're separate from God due to the condition of spiritual death. As noted in Chapter One and Two, this doesn't mean that they don't have a spirit but rather that their spirit is dead to God and therefore having a relationship with the Creator is impossible. No human effort—no religion—can change this condition, which is why Jesus answered his disciples' inquiry about obtaining salvation thusly: "With man this is impossible, but not with God; all things are possible with God" (Mark 10:26-27). It is impossible for human religion to save people from eternal death and reconcile them to God. People can only be saved through the LORD's prescribed method of salvation—spiritual regeneration via the gospel (John 3:3,6 & Titus 3:5).

Until this happens they are "in the darkness," spiritually speaking. Why? Because we can only "see light" by being "in" God's light, as this passage shows:

> **For with you [God] is the fountain of life;**
> **in your light we see light.**
>
> **Psalm 36:9**

> **For you are the fountain of life, the light**
> **by which we see.**
>
> **Psalm 36:9** (NLT)

God *is* the Fountain of Life from which all life flows so it's necessary to hook up with Jehovah in order to receive spiritual life. Why do you think Christ said "I have come so that [you] may have life and have it to the full" (John 10:10)? So if you want God's abundant life flowing in your life it's through Christ and his New Covenant message, not Mohammad, Confucius, Buddha or Sciencefictionology.

This isn't to say, by the way, that every person who says they're a Christian is in the light. Any deviation from biblical truth is darkness even if the person or group *says* they're Christian, like Mormons. In fact, John is addressing *believers* in 1 John 2:9-11 and plainly says to *believers* that if any of them hates their brother or sister in the Lord they're still **in the darkness**. So someone can be a part of a church fellowship, say they're a Christian and even be in a position of authority, like a pastor, and actually be in the darkness, which is STAGE ONE.

The fact that those in STAGE ONE are "in the darkness" explains why we see intelligent and otherwise moral people supporting so-called gay marriage and the mass-murder of unborn children. It's why they support the free speech of every group, even Muslims, but not biblical Christians. It explains why good is now considered bad and evil is now good (Isaiah 5:20). It's why the president of the USA will call a practicing homosexual and congratulate him for an openly sinful lifestyle, but puts genuine Christians on terror-watch lists.

This is why the passage refers to people in STAGE ONE as figuratively blind and therefore not knowing where they're going. Because they're separate from their Creator they don't comprehend the meaning of life, at least not in a spiritual sense or eternal scope. Generally speaking, life to them is limited to this temporal world. Their basic attitude is "Let us eat and drink, for tomorrow we die" and so their lives reflect this limited mindset one way or another (1 Corinthians 15:32 & Isaiah 22:13).

Hating Others—Carnal Hostility

Lastly, hatred is a characteristic of those in STAGE ONE, which—again—isn't to suggest that *everyone* in this stage actively hates others. John simply says, by the Holy Spirit, that Christians who actively hate their brothers and sisters in Christ are "in the darkness," that is, still stuck in STAGE ONE. This includes those who constantly badmouth believers through gossip, slander, mocking and negative spinning. Why do you think Proverbs 26:28 says "A lying tongue *hates* those it hurts"? Because it's true! Those who utilize their tongues as weapons against others— usually behind their backs—do so because they are hostile, envious or rivalrous of the people they're attacking. In short, they *hate* them.

I should point out that I know people who are in STAGE ONE (because they're not in Christ and are therefore spiritually unregenerated), but they genuinely don't walk in hatred, at least as far as I can tell. They're even tolerant and accepting of believers and the Christian message. Such people could be considered high level STAGE ONE with a foothold in the other stages in a substitutionary sense, as detailed last chapter.

Too often, however, I observe libertines give lip service to tolerance, but refuse to tolerate the biblical perspective because it's offensive to them and therefore they regard believers as "bigots," which seems to be their favorite word (rolling my eyes). This reveals their hatred—their hostility or enmity—toward Jesus Christ and genuine believers. It's ironic that "bigot" is their favorite word because *they're* bigots! Whether they know it or not, they're "in the darkness."

You'll notice that I qualified hatred in this section as "carnal hostility." Let me explain. There is such a thing as righteous enmity. For instance, Hebrews 10:13 references Christ's "enemies" who will eventually be made his "footstool." 'Enemies' in the Greek is *echthros (ech-THROS)*, which is where we get the feminine *echthra (EKH-thrah)* translated as "hatred" in Paul's list of works of the flesh in Galatians 5:19-21. So there's such a thing as righteous hostility or righteous enmity; and this explains passages that say point blank that the LORD hates the arrogant, the violent, etc. (e.g. Psalm 5:5 & 11:5). The wages of sin is death, which God must ultimately execute on those who reject his gracious offer of reconciliation and eternal life through the gospel; that is, those who refuse to repent (Acts 20:21). This is the "second death" that the unrepentant will face where "raging fire will consume the enemies of God" (Revelation 20:13-15 & Hebrews 10:26-27). Notice that those who refuse to repent are called the "enemies of God." They're God's enemies by their own choice

(James 4:4). The LORD must carry out this "second death" because He's perfectly just; and divine justice demands the execution of the penalty of sin. However, God is also love, which is why He's offering a way out for sinners; i.e. redemption. He doesn't "want anyone to perish, but everyone to come to repentance" (2 Peter 3:9). "For God so loved the world that he gave his one and only Son, that whoever believes in him shall not perish but have eternal life" (John 3:16).

The reason I'm going into a little detail on this is because most believers are ignorant of these biblical truths and don't realize that enmity can be righteous and justified. Did you know that the LORD loves justice and hates crime (Isaiah 61:8)? This explains why He ordains human governments to punish wrongdoers; that is, criminals (Romans 13:1-4). Believers are called to imitate God and therefore we are to love justice and hate crime as well, which involves seeing to it that criminals are apprehended and punished according to the God-ordained governing authorities.

However, carnal hostility (hatred) is different. It's rooted in enmity based on arrogance, envy, jealousy and rivalry, which are all works of the flesh. People who regularly and unrepentantly walk in carnal hostility are "in the darkness"—STAGE ONE— even those who *say* they're believers. That's what John was getting across in 1 John 2:9-11.

STAGE TWO: Childhood

The Holy Spirit via John refers to STAGE TWO as the childhood stage of spirituality. This has nothing to do with the physical age of the person. Someone could be 90 years-old and be a child spiritually. My dad, for instance, didn't get saved until his late 60s when I took him to several evangelistic meetings. He received Christ and was spiritually reborn—transferred from death to life—and his actions confirmed it. He just wept and wailed at every service throughout the worship and, again, during the closing altar call. The LORD ministered to his heart with His potent healing touch. It's was incredible. While Dad was in his late 60s he was merely a child spiritually.

"Infants in Christ"

Infancy is the earliest level of STAGE TWO. Notice how Paul describes the believers in Corinth:

> **Brothers and sisters, I could not address you as people who are spiritual but as people who are still worldly—<u>mere infants in Christ</u>. (2) I gave you milk, not solid food, for you were not yet ready for it. Indeed, you are still not ready. (3) You are still worldly. For since there is jealousy and quarreling among you, are you not worldly? Are you not acting like mere humans? (4) For when one says, "I follow Paul," and another, "I follow Apollos," are you not mere human beings?**
>
> **1 Corinthians 3:1-4**

This was a soft rebuke to the Corinthian Christians because they had not yet even learned to live by the spirit and therefore weren't producing the fruits of the spirit, at least not on a consistent basis (Galatians 5:22-23). Instead, they were walking in jealousy and the corresponding quarreling. They were flesh-ruled, not spirit-controlled. Moreover, they were developing a spirit of rigid sectarianism—faction-ism—where different believers favored different teachers and refused to receive from anyone else. As noted in the previous chapter, this is a tell-tale sign of people in STAGE TWO. Do you see people who are extremely sectarian about their church/sect/ministry and who refuse to receive from genuine ministers outside their camp? Sometimes they won't even acknowledge them as legitimate fellow believers (!). Make no mistake, such people are mere infants in Christ.

Infants in Christ would appear on the Four Stages diagram like so:

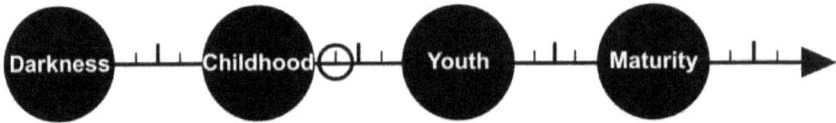

Notice what Paul said about infants in this passage:

> **So Christ himself gave the <u>apostles</u>, the <u>prophets</u>, the <u>evangelists</u>, the <u>pastors</u> and <u>teachers</u>, (12) to <u>equip his people for works of service</u>, so that the body of Christ may be <u>built up</u> (13) until we all reach unity in the faith and in the knowledge of the Son of God and <u>become mature</u>, attaining to the whole measure of the fullness of Christ.**
> **(14) <u>Then we will no longer be infants, tossed back and forth by the waves, and blown here and there by every wind of teaching</u> and by the cunning and craftiness of people in their deceitful scheming.**
> **Ephesians 4:11-14**

The fivefold ministry gifts are apostle, prophet, evangelist, pastor and teacher. The purpose of these anointings or callings is **1.** to "equip" God's people for "works of service," meaning to prepare them for works of ministry, **2.** to "build up" believers, and **3.** to help Christians "become mature." With this understanding, consider ministers who do the precise opposite: (1.) they don't prepare believers for works of ministry, (2.) they tear them down rather than build them up and (3.) they encourage spiritual immaturity, including dependency *on* the pastoral staff, rather than maturity indicated by independence *from* the pastoral staff. "Ministers" who do this aren't fulfilling their commission and are therefore ignorant or, at worst, counterfeit.

Verse 14 shows what results when fivefold ministers perform their calling properly: Believers will **no longer be infants**, but instead become mature and, as such, will no longer be "tossed back and forth by the waves, and blown here and there by every wind of teaching." What's this indicate? Physical infants in the natural are completely dependent on their parents or guardians and have no wise parameters except those provided by their caregivers. In my local area an infant wandered off and disappeared from the yard; they found his body nearby in an old uncovered well. Infant believers are like this. The ministers of their fellowship act as spiritual parents, which is why Paul referred to himself as the Corinthians' "father" (1 Corinthians 4:15). Spiritual parents nurture those in STAGE TWO through the milk of God's Word and, as they grow, solid food. Those who are at the infancy level can only handle milk, which is why Paul called the Corinthians "infants" and said: "I gave you milk, not solid food, for you were not yet ready for it" (1 Corinthians 3:1-2). It's through the milk of the Word and, eventually, the meat of the Word that a spiritual foundation is established in believers' lives.

Because those at the early levels of STAGE TWO lack a spiritual foundation it's easy for them to be "tossed back and forth... and blown here and there by every wind of teaching." Paul wrote the epistle of Ephesians a mere three decades after Christ's resurrection and at that early juncture of the Church there were already all kinds of contradicting teachings spread by immature or misguided Christians and quasi-Christians, just like there are today.

Those who go on to spiritual maturity, however, aren't blown here and there by every wind of teaching. This doesn't mean they put God in a box and are unopen to revelation from the Word;

it just means they won't allow contradicting teachings to make them spiritually unstable. If they come across something they haven't heard before they'll investigate it in detail, like the Bereans in Acts 17:10-12. They'll only receive that which they discern is thoroughly and clearly supported by the Scriptures. By doing this they protect themselves from false doctrine and also keep their spiritual walk from stagnating due to the lack of fresh revelation, which simply means more accurate data from God's Word and the understanding thereof.

We'll look at the biblical way to establish a surefire spiritual foundation in <u>Chapter Nine</u> and <u>Ten</u>.

"Children" only Relate to God in a Daddy Sense

Let's now go back and reread John's brief description of those in the childhood stage:

> **(12) I am writing to you, dear <u>children</u>, because <u>your sins have been forgiven</u> on account of his name…**
> **(14) I write to you, dear <u>children</u>, because <u>you know the Father.</u>**
> **1 John 2:12,14**

These verses describe those in the childhood stage in two simple ways: **1.** Their sins have been forgiven, and **2.** they know God as their Father. Concerning the first, the sins of those in STAGE TWO are forgiven because they embraced the message of Christ and received the forgiveness of sins through spiritual regeneration:

> **For he has rescued us from <u>the dominion of darkness</u> and brought us into the kingdom of the Son he loves, (14) in whom we have redemption, <u>the forgiveness of sins</u>.**
>
> Colossians 1:13-14

Being "rescued from the dominion of darkness" refers to leaving STAGE ONE; and being "brought into the kingdom of the Son" refers to finding sanctuary in STAGE TWO as a child of God, obtaining "redemption, the forgiveness of sins."

Concerning knowing God as their Father: Those in the childhood stage only know God as their father; that is, in the sense of a parent. Why? Because, spiritually speaking, they *are* children and, as such, it's only natural that they relate to God strictly in a parental sense. This will change, of course, as they grow and come to know the LORD in many other ways. We can relate it to our physical childhood: When we were infants we only knew our parents as parents—Mommy & Daddy. As we grew, however, we started to know them in other ways—as rulers of the household, friends, comforters, teachers, payers of allowance when we fulfilled our responsibilities, guides into adulthood, etc. As our relationships grew it didn't negate the fact that they were still our parents, it just opened the door for us to know them in other, deeper ways. It's the same with our relationship with the Almighty. As infants and young children we only know God as a parent. How do immature children regard their parents? As providers. In other words, they think of them in terms of what they can give them. It's an immature "gimme, gimme" mentality that God wants believers to eventually grow out of but, unfortunately, too many never do. This immature mindset is why so many people automatically think of asking for things—petition—when they think of prayer. In reality petition is a miniscule aspect of prayer. Yes, it's a type of prayer, but prayer—communion with God—is so much more than just petition! As we develop spiritually we come to know the

LORD in so many other ways than merely Daddy who gives us things. We come to know Him as our friend (John 15:14-15), our guide (John 16:13), our Comforter/Helper (John 15:26), our faithful deliverer (Psalm 144:2), the King of kings (Revelation 19:16), the Supreme Judge (James 4:12), the awe-inspiring Creator of all things (Revelation 10:6) and so on.

The fact that John refers to believers in STAGE TWO as "children" reveals why I decided to primarily refer to the stages in terms of "STAGE ONE," "STAGE TWO," and so forth in this book. After all, no one wants to be referred to as a child, particularly men; so utilizing the 'stages' terminology eliminates this issue.

STAGE THREE: Youth

Let's now consider how the Holy Spirit through John refers to those in STAGE THREE, the youth stage of spiritual growth:

> **I write to you, young men,**
> **because you are strong,**
> **and the word of God lives in you,**
> **and you have overcome the evil one.**
> **1 John 2:14b**

John describes those in the youth stage as **1.** being strong, **2.** the Word of God lives in them, and **3.** they have overcome the evil one (which is also stated in verse 13). Let's consider all three.

"You are Strong and the Word of God Lives in You"

Those in STAGE THREE are strong because they've successfully gone through the "Christian boot camp" of STAGE

TWO. A spiritual foundation has been established and they therefore have stability in their Christian walk, at least as far as not being blown this way and that way by every wind of doctrine, as is typical of STAGE TWO.

The Word of God lives in them not only through the *living* Word (1 Peter 1:23), but the *written* Word now dwells in their hearts through the feeding they received in STAGE TWO from quality pastors and teachers, not to mention their own studies with the help of the Holy Spirit. The latter, by the way, is a characteristic of STAGE THREE, which shows that a STAGE TWO believer who regularly studies God's Word is simultaneously growing in STAGE THREE. This is the way it's supposed to be: **No matter where we're at in the Four Stages we shouldn't be stagnant. We should always be progressing to the next stage or the next level of the stage we're in. This creates momentum and an unstoppable spirit.**

"You Have Overcome the Evil One"

Those in STAGE THREE "have overcome the evil one" in more ways than spiritual rebirth and salvation from eternal damnation, which are applicable in STAGE TWO. Through the Word that they've learned and the discipline they've acquired with the supervision of their pastors they've overcome the flesh. Remember the flesh is the sinful nature and could also be called the satanic nature because anyone who practices the desires of the flesh is not only living *for* the devil, but living *like* the devil.

They've also "overcome the evil one" because they've escaped another one of his favorite traps—legalism. What exactly is legalism? It's the belief and practice that eternal salvation can be attained through obedience to religious law or good works. That's the common definition. Its broader definition has to do with its root word **legal,** which of course refers to law or rules. Legal-ism could hence be called law-ism or rule-ism. It's the *obsession* with moral or religious laws and therefore legalists primarily judge others based on strict adherence to the rules they deem important, many of them being unbiblical. Furthermore, legal-ism emphasizes the *letter of the law* rather than its spirit.

You could say that legalism is the mentality that godliness is an outward job. Hence, legalists focus on the outer at the expense of the inner. To them a person's outward façade is more important than the inward reality. For instance, as long as an individual goes to every church service throughout the week, and all that goes with it—wearing the "right" dress clothes, carrying the Bible, saying "Amen" at the appropriate moment, putting something in the offering, seeking the favor of the pastor, etc.—it's okay to be a malicious, lying, envious, arrogant, blustering, abusive, sexually immoral, gossiping, slanderous, drunken, chattering fool the rest of the time (not that any one person would likely be *all* these things). Simply put, legalism is religious hypocrisy. It's putting on an act. It's *fake* Christianity.

It's easy to fall into the rut of legalism in STAGE TWO if you're not progressing forward with a finger or hand in the next two stages. This is especially so if you go to a fellowship where the pastoral staff foolishly encourages ongoing dependency. Believers who genuinely advance to STAGE THREE have escaped this huge satanic pitfall. For anyone who argues that legalism isn't satanic, remember what Jesus said to the Pharisees, the quintessential example of legalism in the Bible: The Pharisees claimed that God was their Father, but Jesus plainly told them they were children of the devil, the father of lies (John 8:41-44). In other words, they were counterfeits.[8]

---

[8] For more information on legalism see my 2013 book *Legalism Unmasked*.

STAGE THREE "Boot Camp"

We've talked about the "boot camp" of STAGE TWO, but STAGE THREE has its own boot camp. It's not like boot camp in STAGE TWO, which is experienced with others within the institution and under the supervision of pastors. STAGE THREE boot camp is where you are sent to the "desert" and it's just you and God. Some good biblical examples include Joseph, Moses, Job, Naomi, Ruth, David, Daniel, Jeremiah, Jesus Christ and Paul. They all went through such a wilderness "boot camp." Take Moses, for instance, he was exiled to the desert for forty years where he prepared to be used of God to deliver the Israelites from Egypt, which was his figurative "promised land." The Hebrews whom Moses delivered went through their own wilderness experience before they entered their literal promised land and many didn't make it due to unbelief and a spirit of fear. The ones who made it, Joshua and Caleb, did so because they had a "different spirit," a spirit of bold faith (Numbers 14:24,30). Every believer who successfully "graduates" to STAGE THREE will have their own wilderness experience. As long as you have a spirit of faith and endurance, like Joshua and Caleb, you'll eventually enter your "promised land."[9] This is why the Holy Spirit encourages us in the Word to "imitate those who through faith and patience inherit what has been promised" (Hebrews 6:12). It's not just faith, but faith **and** patience, which is perseverance or endurance. We'll look at this more in Chapter Seven.

Things to keep in mind about your wilderness experience:

---

[9] By the way, "The promised land" is *not* figurative of the believer's eternal state (or "heaven"), as some erroneously suggest. After all, there were hostile nations and giants in the promised land and there will be no such conflict in the new heavens and new earth (2 Peter 3:13). The "promised land" is figurative of walking in the blessings of your covenant and fulfilling the dreams/courses/ assignments the Holy Spirit puts on your heart as you seek the LORD (see Chapter Six for details on how to discern and attain *your* promised land).

- If you want the mountaintop you'll have to go through the valley.
- If you want the oasis, you'll have to go through the desert.
- If you want spiritual power, you'll need to flex your spiritual muscles in the wilderness.
- If you want to walk in the realm of the impossible, you must to be willing to walk in faith with the LORD in impossible situations.

The fact that 1 John 2:14 describes those in STAGE THREE as "strong" believers in whom "the word of God lives in" them and they "have overcome the evil one" shows that those who use STAGE THREE as an excuse to regress to STAGE ONE never truly entered STAGE THREE. They really just fell back to STAGE ONE. There could be a number of reasons for this: **1.** Their own folly, **2.** they unwisely left STAGE TWO prematurely or **3.** they failed to establish a quality spiritual foundation in STAGE TWO due to ineffective or counterfeit "ministry."

While STAGE THREE can be an exhilarating phase in your spiritual journey due to the increased independence, freedoms and responsibilities, it can also be difficult, just like the teenage years and early 20s are sometimes tough. This is due to its inherent growth pangs and awkwardness.

One thing that's great about STAGE THREE—even exciting—is that you get to inspect the foundation that was laid in STAGE TWO in view of God's Word and the counsel of the Holy Spirit. It's where you "eat the meat and spit out the bones" in regards to what you learned in STAGE TWO. While this process is difficult as well, it's also thrilling and inspiring as you adjust your foundation and make repairs in light of more accurate and biblically balanced information. Believers who fail to do this never truly graduate from STAGE TWO because they're locked in a faction-ist mode. Of course, this doesn't mean they can't have a foot or hand in STAGE THREE or FOUR while stuck in STAGE TWO, but this will be the limit of their spiritual growth due to the infection of rigid sectarianism, i.e. faction-ism.

STAGE FOUR: Maturity (Parenthood)

Let's now look at how the Holy Spirit via John describes believers in STAGE FOUR:

> **I am writing to you, fathers,**
>> **because <u>you know him</u> who is from the beginning...**
>
> **I am writing to you, fathers,**
>> **because <u>you know him</u> who is from the beginning**
>>> **1 John 2:13,14**

John refers to believers in STAGE FOUR twice in 1 John 2 and, as you can see, the same way both times. Those in STAGE FOUR are "fathers" because **1.** it's the spiritual stage of adulthood or maturity, and **2.** it's the stage where believers are able to reproduce and properly rear other believers, that is, disciple them. Those in STAGE THREE are also able to reproduce, of course, but they're not mature enough to effectively disciple converts, which is why new believers need to hook up with a ministry where they'll be exposed to mature believers—believers in STAGE FOUR—who can function as spiritual fathers or mothers, like Paul was with the Corinthians (1 Corinthians 4:15). These mature believers can properly disciple them, which includes establishing a sound foundation for them through the "ministry of the Word" (Acts 6:1-4).

I should add that believers at any stage or level can theoretically help less mature believers get to where they are spiritually. For instance, someone at high-level STAGE TWO can help someone at low-level STAGE TWO and someone at mid-level STAGE THREE can assist someone at high-level STAGE TWO. This corresponds to the axiom: **You can only give what you've got. If you don't have it, you can't give it.** If you're not in STAGE FOUR you can't help someone get there. This works in the natural as well as the spiritual. I'm of course talking about helping people get to a higher *spiritual* level and not assisting them in some other way, like giving money or food, or performing a good deed, like fixing an appliance. Anyone can do these types of things for anyone regardless of their stage/level, as long as they have the physical means or skills to do so.

Knowing God beyond just Daddy

Now observe how John describes mature believers as "knowing Him who is from the beginning." This is different than those in STAGE TWO—the childhood stage—who only know God as their Father. Those in STAGE FOUR, by contrast, know the LORD as the One who "is from the beginning." In other words, they know Him in a deeper fashion, in a more eternal sense. Think about it in terms of how you knew your natural father as a child and contrast that with how you know (or knew) him as an adult. As a child you just knew him as Dad, the one who works, makes money and gives you things. As an adult you know him in a much deeper way: You know the details of what he does (or did) for a living, you know his history and his dreams, you know him as a friend. It's the same thing with the LORD. When you transfer into STAGE THREE and, especially, STAGE FOUR you come to know God in such a deeper way than when you simply knew Him as your dad in STAGE TWO. The same goes for the Holy Spirit and Jesus Christ. All three are one, but separate (Matthew 28:19 & 2 Corinthians 13:14).

The differences between believers' perception of God in STAGE TWO and STAGE FOUR can be observed in their attitude toward prayer. Believers in STAGE TWO are children, spiritually speaking, and therefore perceive the LORD in a parental sense, as their Daddy. There's nothing wrong with this as it simply reflects where they're at spiritually. However, because their perception of God is limited to a parental role they regard prayer accordingly. Hence, prayer to them is mainly asking for things that they need or desire. This is petition, which is certainly a form of prayer (Matthew 7:7-11), but it's only one of several types of prayer, and one of the minor ones at that, at least as you mature. Jesus said that believers who learn to seek God first—not only, but first—will automatically have their needs met, which frees up their prayer time for more important things (Matthew 6:25-33).

Believers in STAGE FOUR view prayer as what it is—communion with the Creator—an occasion to hook up with the very Fountain of Life and receive the life, light and empowerment thereof (Psalm 36:9), not to mention help others through intercession.

The Different Types of Prayer

Prayer simply means communion with God—it's *talking with* your Creator. Jesus' disciples asked him *how* to pray and this was his response:

"This then is how you should pray:

Our Father in heaven,
hallowed be your name,
your kingdom come,
your will be done on earth as it is in
heaven.
Give us today our daily bread.
Forgive us our debts, as we also have forgiven
our debtors.

And lead us not into temptation, but deliver us from the evil one.
For yours is the kingdom and the power and the glory forever. Amen"

Matthew 6:9-13

This is typically referred to as "the Lord's prayer" and people sometimes pray it word-for-word, particularly when the occasion calls for a ritualistic or brief prayer to open or close ceremonies. This is fine, but it's really not a prayer to be spoken by rote. "The Lord's prayer" is actually **an *outline* of different types of prayer**. In other words, it's **a prayer *skeleton*** that needs to be filled in with the "flesh" of our spontaneous prayers according to our unique expressions, communion, needs or desires and the specific people and situations touching us. The outline can be broken down as such:

- "Our Father in heaven" = Communion or fellowship with God.
- "Hallowed be your name" = Praise & worship.
- "Your kingdom come, your will be done on earth as it is in heaven" = Binding & loosing or intercession, that is, releasing God's will and kingdom into people's lives and situations on earth, including your own.
- "Give us today our daily bread" = Petition, that is, praying for your needs and righteous desires.
- "Forgive us our debts as we also have forgiven our debtors" = Repentance, venting, and forgiveness where applicable.
- "And lead us not into temptation, but deliver us from the evil one" = Armoring up, protection, watchfulness, speaking in faith, and deliverance.
- "For yours is the kingdom and the power and the glory forever. Amen" = Return to praise and close.

As you can see, each part of "the Lord's Prayer" refers to a specific type of prayer. Let's look at four of them a little closer:

"Our Father in heaven" refers to communion with God since the believer is addressing God as his or her "Father." 'Father' indicates *familial* relation and relationship requires communication, hence fellowship. Christianity at its core is a *relationship* with the Creator of the universe, which is why the gospel is referred to as the *message of reconciliation* in 2 Corinthians 5:18-20. I encourage all believers to cultivate an intimate relationship with their heavenly Father where you're in constant communion throughout the day, even when you're in bed (Psalm 63:6). Paul referred to this as "praying without ceasing" (1 Thessalonians 5:17 KJV) and the "fellowship of the Holy Spirit" (2 Corinthians 13:14).

"Hallowed be your name" refers to praise & worship. To 'hallow' means to honor as holy and venerate, that is, treat with respect and reverence. God's name—YaHWeH—represents the Creator Himself so we are to hallow the Great "I Am" (Exodus 3:13-14). The only way you can accomplish this in prayer is by *telling* him. Praise is celebration and includes thanksgiving, raving and boasting, whereas worship is adoration. Praise naturally attracts God's presence and is in accordance with the law of respect: What you respect moves toward you while what you don't respect moves away from you. Worship, on the other hand, is adoration or awe, and is the response to being *in* His presence. See Psalm 95:1-7 and Psalm 100 for verification.

We could further differentiate praise & worship as such: Praise celebrates God whereas worship humbly reveres Him; praise lifts God up while worship bows when He is lifted; praise dances before God whereas worship pulls off His shoes; praise extols God for what He's done while worship adores Him for who He is; praise says "Praise the Lord" whereas worship demonstrates that He is Lord; praise is thanksgiving for being a co-heir in Christ while worship lays the crown at His feet.

Every believer is called to deeper praise & worship. It will literally *revolutionize* your life, as it has mine and continues to do so. For more details on praise & worship see the section in Chapter Eleven: *A Living Sacrifice in Worship*.

"Your kingdom come, your will be done on earth as it is in heaven." This is not talking about praying for Jesus' return and the set-up of his kingdom on earth, whether in the Millennium or eternally, it's talking about the principle of binding & loosing in this "present evil age." This means *now*. Do you want God's kingdom to reign in your life and the lives of others? You have to *release* it through prayer. Do you want God's will to be done in your life and the lives of others? You have to *loose* it via prayer. In other words, *God's kingdom will not come and reign on this earth unless a believer releases it through prayer and action; and God's will is not done on earth unless the church looses His will via prayer and action.* Simply put, believers have the power to bind the kingdom of darkness and loose the kingdom of light. See Matthew 16:19 & 18:18-19.[10]

"Forgive us our debts, as we also have forgiven our debtors." When in prayer believers need to be honest and transparent with their Creator. He knows everything anyway so you might as well be transparent. Only a fool would attempt to hide something from the all-knowing Almighty. Cultivate and maintain a humble, pliable heart that's open to correction. We need to always be willing to search our hearts—our attitudes, motives and actions—and make adjustments where necessary. Never put off repentance; make it a priority. This keeps our spiritual arteries clear and life flowing, whereas unconfessed sin will clog them up and block God's power. Humility attracts God's favor and He

---

[10] The principle of binding & loosing is covered in detail in the teaching "Spiritual Warfare—the Basics" at the Fountain of Life website, as well as chapter 7 of *The Believer's Guide to Forgiveness & Warfare*.

forgives the repentant. Similarly, we need to extend grace to those who sin against us and humbly repent. That's what this type of prayer refers to: forgiving those we *should* forgive. It shouldn't be misinterpreted to mean we're obligated to forgive everyone for everything all the time, no conditions whatsoever, because Jesus didn't teach this and the Bible doesn't support it. Take, for instance, the unrepentant brother in Jesus' illustration from Matthew 18:15-17. Since the man refused to repent Jesus instructed that his sin should be held against him: He was to be dis-fellowshipped and regarded as a non-believer until he repents. Paul dealt with a real-life situation like this and instructed the Corinthians to do the same (1 Corinthians 5:1-5). Thankfully, the man later repented and so Paul encouraged the believers to warmly welcome him back into their fellowship (2 Corinthians 2:6-11). Luke 17:3-4 is another example.[11]

The other types of prayer from Jesus' outline are self-explanatory and I encourage you to practice and develop in each area.

Communing with God

Let's focus on the first two types of prayer: Communion with God and praise & worship. It's no accident that these are the first two kinds of prayer Jesus mentions in his outline (Matthew 6:9-13). They're simply the most important. After all, what does the average father or mother want to hear from their children, particularly as the children grow and develop? Not, "Gimme, gimme," but rather simple communion: "Hi Dad! How are you doing today? You're awesome!" "Do you have time? I'd like to just hang out with you." "Mother, I have something I've been

---

[11] See my 2012 book *The Believer's Guide to Forgiveness & Warfare* for important details on this topic, particularly chapter 4.

thinking a lot about and I'd like to share it with you to see what you think." "Mom, you're so beautiful!" "Dad, tell me more about that project you're working on in the yard; it's lookin' great so far." Etcetera. If this is the kind of communion our earthly parents prefer why would we think it's any different with our heavenly Father?

You can have these types of conversations with God throughout the day, every day—when you wake up in bed, when you're in the shower, when you're driving, when you're walking down the hall, in the evening, etc. As noted earlier, Paul referred to this as "praying without ceasing" (1 Thessalonians 5:17 KJV) and the "fellowship of the Holy Spirit" (2 Corinthians 13:14). We have to get away from the idea that we only encounter God when we go to church gatherings once or twice a week. This is an Old Testament mentality.

Although the Holy Spirit was active among the Israelites in Old Testament times, it was much different than the way it is with believers in the New Testament. The Holy Spirit's work in that earlier era was limited and selective because the Israelites were spiritually un-regenerated. However, they did have a covenant with God and there are glimmerings of what the Spirit's function would be in the new covenant. David, for instance, was a type of the New Testament believer. Yet there was no spiritual rebirth, no indwelling and no baptism of the Spirit, at least not in the thorough scale we enjoy today. Simply put, the Israelites were *not* temples of the Holy Spirit as believers are in the new covenant because they weren't spiritually regenerated. The temple of God was a literal temple—a building—and before that, a tent tabernacle. Both the Tabernacle of Moses and the Temple of Solomon housed God's presence via the Ark of the Covenant (Exodus 25:22). These structures were literally God's house (although His presence was hidden in the Holy of Holies where the Ark was located, and the High Priest would only enter once a year). For the Israelites to encounter God they literally had to go to the Tabernacle or

Temple, but—Praise God—this isn't the way it is in the New Testament period because believers are literally the temples of God through spiritual rebirth (1 Corinthians 3:16)!

So attending church gatherings at a church facility is not the primary way to connect with God in the New Testament era, although it is *a way* due to the corporate anointing, which Jesus spoke of in Matthew 18:20, not to mention the anointing of fivefold ministry gifts, detailed in Ephesians 4:11-13. Experiencing this "corporate anointing," however, doesn't require going to a specific *building*. It can take place wherever believers meet—a park, a street corner, the mall, someone's house, a vehicle, the workplace, etc. Even better: Since every believer is the temple of God in this New Covenant period we can encounter the LORD every day. If you're not doing it already, I encourage you to get in the habit of fellowshipping with the LORD on a continual basis, 24/7. It'll revolutionize your walk.

Communing with God in Solitary Places

There's a difference between the 24/7 fellowship noted above and personal prayer sessions. Regarding the latter, Jesus said "when you pray, go into your room, close the door and pray to your Father, who is unseen. Then your Father, who sees what is done in secret, will reward you" (Matthew 6:6). Jesus was simply talking about finding a solitary place for prayer sessions, known only to you and the LORD. This is in contrast to religious hypocrites who love to pray in front of others, which really isn't communion with God, but rather putting on a show to impress people, which is fakeness, (Matthew 6:5). 'Hypocrite' literally means "actor." This isn't to say, by the way, that it's wrong to pray with other believers, as is shown in the Bible (Acts 12:12), just that' it's wrong for believers to pray in front of others for the purpose of impressing them and proving how supposedly godly they are.

When Jesus said to "go into your room, close the door and pray" he was simply talking about finding a solitary place where it's just you and the LORD. It's interesting that Jesus "as was his habit" often went to solitary places in the wilderness to pray, as shown in Mark 1:35, Matthew 14:23 and Luke 22:39-41. How come? Because there's something about nature that's conducive to encountering the Creator.

I think this is why men in particular are attracted to outdoor activities—like hunting, hiking, kayaking, fishing, etc.—because on some primal level they encounter God who is revealed in creation (Psalm 19:1-4, 97:6 & Romans 1:20).

Let me bring something up that all hard-working ministers can relate to: Recently someone insinuated that it must be great to be a full-time minister because of all the supposed time off. I just smiled and allowed him to continue in his arrogant ignorance (although my wife humbly spoke of the constant work and devotion necessary for serving in full-time ministry). The guy simply wasn't aware of what it takes to run a world outreach ministry, including the determination and focus it takes to write books that are often over 250 pages.

Later that night the Holy Spirit ministered to me and said that the man was ignorant of what it took to even start a world-reaching ministry let alone run one. Images flashed through my mind of literal *years* going out to pray in wilderness areas North, South, East and West of my home, seeking the LORD and interceding, etc. This was well before I even intended to start a ministry. Often I would drive an hour to get to a good spot, sometimes 90 minutes or more. Images of these prayer locations and the sweet communion I had with the Lord flashed through my mind. Of course, this man was completely unaware of all this because I never informed him. Jesus said to keep your prayer sessions to yourself and God. I'm only sharing it here as **1.** an *example* to believers (1 Peter 5:1-4) and **2.** to illustrate that those who seek the LORD will find Him (Jeremiah 29:13). As you make the LORD first priority—not your *only* priority, but the *first* priority (Matthew 6:33)—He'll "direct your paths" (Proverbs 3:5-6).

Do you want an easy-to-understand scriptural way to discern God's will and fulfill it in any stage or level of spiritual growth? See <u>Chapter Six</u>.

PART II

Tools for Spiritual Growth

What good is it to know the Four Stages of Spiritual Growth if you don't have the tools necessary to grow and mature? That's what PART II is all about—providing the tools you'll need to successfully go on to spiritual maturity; and continue growing. In other words, whereas PART I shows you where you *are* spiritually and where you need to go, PART II shows you *how to get there!*

Chapter Five

A Disciple is a Humble *Learner*

There's something that's absolutely essential to spiritual growth regardless of what stage or level you're at and it guarantees *continuing* growth. It's so simple it can be overlooked—it's the attitude of a humble *learner*.

Are YOU a Disciple?

It's not wise to cop a 'know it all' spirit because, when people do this, they cease to be learners. This is not good because the Greek word translated as 'disciple'—*mathétés (math-ay-TEEZ)*—means "learner." As such, anyone who's a disciple of Christ must also be a *learner* of Christ, who is "the way, the truth and the life." Even those who are apostles, prophets, evangelists, pastors and teachers in the church are *still* disciples of Christ so they must still be learners; not only learners of the living Word but also the written Word. The Bible shows that both are sources of truth (see John 14:6 & 17:17). **Being a disciple of Christ—a**

learner of God—is a foundational calling that believers will always have, regardless of how far they go in the Lord and how great they are (or become) in the church.

There's a saying: The more you know, the more you know you don't know. The meaning is obvious: The more you acquire knowledge the more you realize the many things you don't know and the innumerable things that remain mysterious and wondrous. This has to do with humility because it takes humility to admit that you don't know something. But religionists infected by legalism become proud of their 'great learning' and consequently become stuffy, know-it-all windbags. Even if someone comes along who shows that they know more on a particular topic or has more understanding, they won't likely admit it or receive from him or her.

Take, for example, Jesus and the Pharisees. Jesus showed these religious leaders over and over that he was more advanced than they were in knowledge, understanding and wisdom, not to mention his great anointing. The Messiah's arguments repeatedly stunned these proud counterfeits to silence. He performed incredible miracles again and again. Yet they were so stubborn they refused to be open to even the possibility that Jesus was more spiritual than they were—that he was perhaps closer to God or that he knew things they didn't.

Nicodemus was the only Pharisee recorded in Scripture who was moved by Jesus' ministry and open to his instruction. He met Yeshua under the cover of darkness for fear of the backlash of his fellow Pharisees (John 3:1-10). On another occasion Nicodemus openly spoke up for Jesus (John 7:45-52) and the Scriptures offer evidence that he ultimately became a believer (John 19:38-42). This is great news for legalists throughout the ages—just because someone's a religious fuddy-duddy functioning within a highly legalistic group doesn't mean he or she has to stay that way!

Arrogance Stops Learning

The question needs to be asked: Why are religionists so stubborn that they can't receive from someone like Jesus or even admit that he was anointed of God? Because sterile religiosity produces arrogance, which is a superiority complex. It looks down on everyone else except other legalists in their organization who are higher up on the "totem pole." Anyone who functions outside of their spiritual tunnel vision, like Jesus did, won't be given the time of day. Why? Because they've already studied within their religious circles and think they have everything down. As far as they're concerned, they already know everything there is to know and you can't give something to someone who thinks they already have everything,

People like Jesus are a threat to the authority and livelihood of stuffy religionists and so must be ignored, discredited or even killed. If the counterfeits can't kill them literally they'll cowardly kill them with words to discredit them by ruining their reputation. It's what arrogant people do. If the Pharisees and other legalists actually dialogued with Jesus it wasn't to learn something spiritual and get closer to God, but rather to somehow trap him in his words so they could denounce him to the people as a violator of God's Word.

If you know elders or leaders in the church who regularly speak ill of legitimate ministers who are diligent and doing wonderful things for the kingdom of God, at least as far as their assignment goes, beware! They're infected by pride and lifeless religiosity.

Be a Learner, not a Spurner

The infection of arrogance can puff-up people so much that they stop being learners in preference to being spurners—always quick to respond to anything outside of their limited prism with scorn, disdain and contempt. Paul said, "Knowledge puffs up, but love builds up. The man who thinks he knows something does not yet know as he ought to know" (1 Corinthians 8:1-2). Paul was well-familiar with this since he used to be a Pharisee named Saul who thought he knew it all about God and Mosaic law. He also thought Jesus Christ was a false teacher and therefore severely persecuted his followers, that is, until Jesus appeared to him on the road to Damascus and humbled his arrogant behind. Saul suddenly discovered that he believed a lie, that his sect wasn't the one true sect and, in fact, they were actually enemies of God!

Think about Paul's words in the above passage and what he was saying between the lines: When we truly start knowing as we ought to know we'll become increasingly aware of our ignorance! True spiritual growth creates a spirit of humility and wonder concerning God and the many mysteries of life whereas religion creates arrogant legalists and rigid sectarians who shut themselves off to greater knowledge and the marvels of the universe. Humility, by contrast, maintains that childlike wonder we need in order to grow spiritually. Reflect on this passage emphasized in Chapter Three: "God opposes the proud but gives his grace to the humble." This Old Testament proverb is quoted by both James and Peter in the New Testament and therefore appears *three times* in the Scriptures (Proverbs 3:34, James 4:6 & 1 Peter 5:5). It goes without saying that the LORD's telling us something of great importance: **God's grace—His favor—only flows to the humble, but he opposes or resists the arrogant**. Think about it.

Every genuine believer is excited about the things of God when they first turn to the LORD, but this sense of awe can gradually wane as they settle into the day-to-day activities of churchianity and everything that goes with it—the expectations, the endless rules (many of them unnecessary, unbiblical and even eye-rolling), the church grind, the constant demands on one's time, etc. Don't get me wrong here, healthy ministries with godly, loving servant-leaders are always good, but experiences with pompous religious people or ministries infected by legalism will sap the life and faith right out of you, unless you're very mature and familiar with spiritual warfare tactics that are Scriptural. ("Spiritual warfare," by the way, simply refers to overcoming evil through spiritual measures, like prayer, blessing, speaking in faith, teaching, valid correction and righteous radicalness).

The Importance of Being Teachable

Paul asked the Roman Christians an important question: "You, then, who teach others, do you not teach yourself?" (Romans 2:21). This is a rhetorical question and so the answer is obvious: Those who are teachers or want to become teachers must be teachable themselves. Why? Because being teachable goes with humility. Proud people think they know it all and are therefore unteachable whereas humble people—no matter how much they know—realize they couldn't possibly know it all and, consequently, remain open to learning and, in fact, continually crave more accurate and enlightening information.

It goes without saying that we need to guard ourselves against an unteachable, know-it-all spirit as we grow in the Lord because this is a characteristic of sterile religionists who **1.** don't really know God as they claim they do, and **2.** have actually ceased from growing spiritually. You heard that right. Anyone who is infected by stubborn arrogance will actually stop growing. Spiritual rigor mortis will set in. Jesus said: "I tell you the truth, anyone who will not receive the kingdom of God like a little child will never enter it" and "the kingdom of God belongs to such as these [children]" (Mark 10:15 & Matthew 19:14). Jesus wasn't encouraging childish behavior, of course, but rather childlike humility, innocence, receptivity, faith and lack of self-sufficiency in regard to God and his kingdom. This is meekness. It attracts God's grace—His favor—whereas arrogance repels him.

Receive from Others

Only a fool refuses to receive from others in their areas of strength. When you need major dental work do you do it yourself or do you go to a reputable dentist? It's the same thing in the kingdom of God. God has provided gifts for the church to equip us for service (ministry) and increase our faith and knowledge; these "gifts" are people who are anointed as pastors, teachers, prophets, etc. (Ephesians 4:11-13). They include people outside of the group with which you're familiar, like Jesus and John the Baptist were to Israelites. Every valid ministry has its areas of expertise and weakness. Take the good and leave the bad (1 Thessalonians 5:21).

Please be sure to maintain your child-like wonder before the LORD as you continue in the faith. No matter how far you go in Christ, no matter how great your calling or works, you'll always be a *learner* of Christ—a **disciple** of the Lord. Yes, even if you're an under-shepherd, a fivefold minister. This will ensure your continuing spiritual growth.

Formal Education and Informal Education

There's this attitude that I sometimes come across that I find perplexing. It's the idea that people are only educated if they have a degree from a college or university. I spent years at a fairly big university and later graduated from a reputable Bible school so I'm well familiar with the hallowed halls of higher learning. As long as you go to class, take notes, regurgitate the material on test day and write the prescribed essays you'll advance and eventually obtain a degree; that is, as long as you have the time and money. The more years you spend and the more money you blow the more advanced your degree.

I'm not against higher education. I'm all for it as long as it contributes to fulfilling your God-given goals, whatever they might be (which we'll address in the next chapter). However, just because someone has a degree doesn't necessarily mean they're educated, particularly in the sense of possessing godly wisdom and Holy Ghost anointing (in fact, the ignorance of some professors is stunning; and in some cases their ignorance is intentional). Nor does *not* having a degree necessarily mean someone's uneducated or lacks wisdom and God's empowerment. John the Baptist and Jesus Christ are Exhibit A. Neither of them had a highfalutin degree and yet they incredibly impacted the world with the anointing of the LORD, particularly the Messiah. John was clothed in camel hair and lived on locusts & wild honey in the desert (Matthew 3:4). Exhibit B would be Jesus' disciples, who were "uneducated, common men" (Acts 4:13). These so-called unschooled ordinary men turned the world upside down! And YOU can too, whether you have an impressive degree or not.

So the Western mentality that people are only authentically educated in the hallowed halls of higher learning is a lie. True education—that is, *learning*—takes place when a person has a humble, teachable heart that thirsts for knowledge and growth. This is a day-to-day education that continues until the day we come "face to face" and "know fully" (1 Corinthians 13:12). (Until then, *no one* knows anything fully, no matter the airs they might put on). I strive daily to be a humble learner; this is what makes my works "studious," as some have called them, not college.

So whether you go to university or not I encourage you to maintain the heart of a learner—a disciple—and be educated daily with the help of the Holy Spirit, our Teacher. Amen.

Chapter Six

How to Obtain Your Desires

In this chapter we're going to look at how to build and maintain constant momentum in your walk with the Lord. It's based on discerning, pursuing and obtaining your desires. I'm not talking about sinful desires, of course, but rather God-given desires. You see, God motivates you by dropping desires in your spirit as you seek Him; and these desires correspond to the works or goals He wants you to fulfill.

People have inquired about my productivity and how I do it. This chapter shows you how and it's based on a simple three-point plan that's thoroughly biblical. I first learned it through a minister in the mid-80s (who I'm sure learned it from someone else and so on) and have been exceedingly grateful ever since because I use it for everything I accomplish. This plan will empower you to be productive in your service for the Lord and obtain your God-given desires.

Focusing on fulfilling the dreams or works the LORD puts in your heart is exciting and creates dynamic propulsion. As you follow the wisdom principles of God's Word you'll become unstoppable in your service for the Lord; and success begats success. It's truly living the "good life" and I don't mean that in a worldly sense.

"The Desire of the Righteous is Only Good"

First we need to establish the difference between righteous desires and unrighteous desires. Notice what the book of wisdom says on this:

> **<u>The desire of the righteous is only good</u>, but the expectation of the wicked is wrath.**
> **Proverbs 11:23** (NASB/KJV)

We'll focus on the first part of the passage since the second part deals with the wicked; unless you're wicked, it doesn't apply to you. The first part plainly says that "the desire of the righteous is only good." If the desire of the righteous is good then the reverse is also true: the desire of **the unrighteous** is *not* good, which would include desires relating to sins like arrogance, adultery, greed or murder. Galatians 5:19-21 provides a good list. How do we learn to distinguish between righteous and unrighteous desires? The Bible shows us how (Hebrews 5:14), which is one of the many reasons it's important to grow in the knowledge of God's Word (Colossians 1:10 & 2 Peter 3:18).

So "the desire of the righteous is only good." 'Desire' here is the Hebrew word *ta'avah (tah-âv-AW)*, which means "that which you earnestly *long* for." It's a desire that **stays with you** and you can't get rid of it. We're talking about a righteous desire, not a wicked one. The Bible says that such a desire is good! Religion has told us for centuries that all desire is bad. No, only evil, sinful desires are bad. **Christianity is not the death of desire—it's the death of selfish and ungodly desire**.

Christians tend to think if they're not called to pastor they're of no value to God. This is a lie straight from the enemy. God is *very* interested in your life. In fact, you're His child through spiritual rebirth (1 John 5:1 & 3:9). Any normal, healthy parent is intensely interested in the life of his/her son or daughter; how much more so your heavenly Father? You must get a hold of the fact that God has strategic purposes for every believer, including YOU. How does He reveal these purposes? **As you make Him first priority He puts burning desires in your heart—** *ta'avahs*—**to motivate you to go in the direction He wants you to go**.

You Were Recreated in Christ to Fulfill the Objectives God Gives You

Notice what this passage says and let it permeate your being:

> **For we are God's [own] handiwork (His workmanship), recreated in Christ Jesus, [born anew] that we may do those <u>good works</u> which God predestined (planned beforehand) for us [<u>taking paths which He prepared ahead of time</u>], that we should walk in them [<u>living the good life</u> which He prearranged and made ready for us to live].**
>
> **Ephesians 2:10** (Amplified)

Every believer is God's "workmanship" "recreated in Christ" to do the good works He planned ahead of time. "Recreated in Christ" is a reference to spiritual regeneration, which takes place when a lost person turns to God in repentance and faith (John 3:3,6 & Acts 20:21). Once you're "recreated in Christ" God has **paths** for you to walk down: "Taking paths which He prepared ahead of time." A good example of this is Paul. God had plans for him to be an apostle even from his mother's womb! (Galatians 1:15).

The Amplified Bible is a paraphrase that amplifies the original Hebrew & Greek. Notice it describes fulfilling the good works the LORD wants us to fulfill in terms of "living the **good life**." You see, **God's will is the best possible path for you to walk**. Being in God's will is exciting because your Creator knows how you're wired—what you can handle and what you can't handle, what excites you and what bores you. Christianity is not dullsville. Religion—including "Christian" religion—might be dullsville but true Christianity isn't. Take believers who are genuinely called to missionary work in developing areas or pastors who pioneer churches. These men and women are dynamic individuals who are excited about their work, despite the hardships and challenges. They're living the "good life."

Some Christians are afraid of God's will because they think it's all doom and gloom. While it's true that the Christian path is filled with trials, temptations and persecutions, God's plan for your life isn't just okay or mediocre, it's good—it's "the **good life**"!

> **The LORD crowns the year with goodness, and <u>God's paths</u> drip with abundance.**
> **Psalm 65:11** (NKJV)

The LORD crowns the year with goodness and His "paths drip with abundance." If God takes you there He'll provide for you there, as long as you endure in faith and don't give up. Jesus said He came that we may have "life to the full," (John 10:10), not mediocre life!

Again, this does not mean there won't be challenges and hardships. Life's a fight, fight it! **You will never outgrow spiritual warfare; you must simply learn to fight.**

The Three-Point Plan

Now we're ready to go over the three-point plan of action. This plan will literally empower you to continually produce during your spiritual sojourn on earth. I'm not talking about a lame formula, but rather ageless principles of wisdom based on the Word of God and the corresponding leading (or inspiration) of the Holy Spirit minute by minute and day to day.

This three-point plan is simple and I use it for *everything* I accomplish in service of the LORD. It works because it's thoroughly biblical and based on the wisdom of God. Let's look at each of the three parts with the understanding that the plan only works for believers who are walking with the Lord and keeping in repentance *à la* Matthew 3:8 and 1 John 1:8-9. Believers who stubbornly refuse to 'fess up when applicable automatically block the flow of God's grace in their lives (James 4:6). It's a simple matter of honesty and humility with your Creator.

1. Acknowledge God and He Will Direct Your Paths

The cornerstone passage for this first part of the plan is this:

> **Trust in the LORD with all your heart and lean not on your own understanding; <u>in all your ways</u>** *<u>acknowledge Him</u>*, **and <u>He will direct your paths</u>.**
>
> **Proverbs 3:5-6**

Acknowledge God in your life and He will *direct* **your paths**. He'll show you where He wants you to go as you seek Him. Simply ask the LORD in prayer to instruct you and teach you in the way you should go. The Bible says that God hears us when we ask according to His will (1 John 5:14) so you can base your request on passages like Proverbs 3:5-6 and this one:

> **"I will instruct you and teach you in the way you should go;**
>
> **I will counsel you with my loving eye on you.**
>
> **(9) Do not be like the horse or the mule, which have no understanding but must be controlled by bit and bridle or they will not come to you."**
>
> **Psalm 32:8-9**

Praying for God's will to be done in your life is in accordance with Jesus' instructions and example (Matthew 6:9-10; 26:39). Keep in mind, however, that the Bible doesn't teach us to seek God *only*, but rather seek Him *first* (Matthew 6:33). In short, we're to make God **first priority**—i.e. sell out to God—but don't get out of balance by seeking God only. That's a ticket to looney religiosity and burnout. Are you with me?

When you acknowledge the LORD in prayer get specific about the area of your life with which you're acknowledging Him. There are different areas to our lives—family, marital, work, devotional, ministerial, educational, recreational, fitness, social, homestead, dating, and so on. What area are you seeking the Creator for guidance?

How exactly does God "direct your path" when you acknowledge Him? By dropping desires in your heart to motivate you. You can't obtain your desires until you know what they are; so get close to the LORD, look deep within, and **draw them out**. This is in line with godly wisdom as shown in Proverbs 20:5: "The purposes of a person's heart are deep waters, but one who has insight draws them out."

You'll have thoughts, ideas or desires concerning a certain area of your life. For instance, you may want to build/buy a house in the country or there may be a certain special person you're thinking about marrying or perhaps you feel called to full-time ministry. Whatever the case, share it with the LORD in prayer, as this verse shows:

> **Roll your works upon the LORD [commit and trust them wholly to Him; <u>He will cause your thoughts to become agreeable to His will,</u> and] so shall your plans be established and succeed.**
>
> **Proverbs 16:3** (Amplified)

When you acknowledge the LORD in prayer He will cause your thoughts to become "agreeable with His will." Please understand that God is your Creator and therefore knows precisely how you tick. As such, He'll guide you according to what you're wired to handle by dropping in your spirit the corresponding desire.

Once you have an earnest desire, keep praying about it to ensure that it's of God (particularly if it's major). **If it's of God it will grow stronger. If not, it'll grow weaker and die out**.

Let me give an example from my own life: In my 20s I constantly wrote songs and recorded them on a four-track recorder. I was also a young Christian and was seeking the LORD with all my heart—studying the Word, praying, attending church services, etc. My main drive beyond God was music. It was my predominant occupational/artistic desire. So I started a band with my best friend, who was a drummer, and we started playing out. We were an overtly Christian band, of course, but after a few years it got old and progress wasn't happening. Beyond that, I was also getting married and seeking the LORD as fervently as ever. Lo and behold my desire to be in a band and compose/play music subsided. Deep inside I knew I needed to break off from the band and, at least, take a break. So that's what I did and, in the ensuing years, God led me to pursue serious ministry (Bible school, regular pulpit sermons, etc.).

You see, I was seeking the LORD—acknowledging Him in my life—and He led me to play in a band for a season, but as I continued seeking Him He moved me to leave that work at the appropriate time. So keep in mind that some things the LORD leads you to do will be seasonal. Jonah's ministry in Nineveh, for example, was seasonal, not forever. It's the same with Paul's work in Corinth. Just because God leads you to do something it doesn't mean it's forever (unless, of course, we're talking about marriage, which is a covenant till death[12]).

Consider this potent passage:

Now to Him who is ABLE to do immeasurably more than all we <u>ask</u> or <u>imagine</u>, according to His power that is at work within us,
Ephesians 3:20

Beloved Christian, you must understand that God will not get involved in your life unless YOU allow Him. He wants to take you places. He's able to do immeasurably more than what you ask or imagine, but are YOU even asking or imagining? How can the LORD do "immeasurably more" if we're not even willing to ask or imagine? The last time I checked God rewards those who earnestly and diligently seek Him, not those who are lazy and apathetic.

This first part of the three-point plan is absolutely essential because it facilitates a purpose-driven life in any stage or level you're at on your spiritual journey. This is imperative to happiness and a sense of meaning (remember Solomon's depressed

---

[12] That is, unless it's impossible to stay married due to unrepentant unfaithfulness or abuse (Matthew 5:32 & 19:9).

commentaries on the meaninglessness of life in Ecclesiastes?). Think about it: If you don't know where you're going you might not like where you end up. If you don't know where you're going, how will you ever know when you get there?

2. <u>Plan</u> Your Way to Meet Your God-Given Objective

Once you have a strong desire—a *ta'avah*—and you know it's God's will, what do you do?

> **<u>The mind of a person plans their way</u>, but the LORD directs their steps.**
> **Proverbs 16:9** (NASB)

God has given you a course—an objective— now you need to *plan* your way in order for the LORD to direct your steps. 'Plan' means "To design or think over." God gave you a **mind** for a reason—use it. I too often see a negative attitude toward the mind in Christian circles (and, by "the mind," I mean the mental realm in general). However, your mind is an awesome gift from your Creator and should be utilized for good. For instance, this proverb shows that you should use your mind to **plan your way**.

Let's say you're seeking the LORD and you discern a strong, persistent desire to be a nurse. This is your God-given course. Now **plan your way** to meet that objective. You can start planning simply by asking the most obvious questions: What nursing schools are available for you to attend? How are you going to apprehend funds? Where are you going to live? Will you work part-time?

When you do this you're planning your way to fulfill your God-given **course** or **objective** utilizing the resources at your disposal. The plan you come up with is your **path** or **way**.

Remember: No one plans to fail, but failures fail to plan.

3. Start Moving toward Your Goal Led of the Holy Spirit

Once you have a general plan then simply **start moving**. In short, it's time for **action**! Get up off your rump and move toward your God-given goal according to the plan you devised. As you do this the LORD will "direct your steps" by the Holy Spirit (Proverbs 16:9).

Discern the difference between **course**, **path** and **steps**:

- Your **course** is your objective, goal, assignment or mission, which is based on the longstanding desire—the *ta'avah*—the LORD gave you as you sought Him.
- Your **path** is the way you planned with your mind to fulfill your course or obtain your goal.
- Your **steps** are you walking down that path day by day utilizing God's direction via the Holy Spirit.

Once you have a goal it's of the utmost importance that you take action and start walking toward it according to your general plan because this will produce **momentum**. As you do this, your goal will increasingly become an obsession, which is good as long as you maintain balance by not neglecting other important areas of your life, like God, sleep, health, recreation[13] and quality relationships. Your God-given goal must become your **main focus** in the area of life for which it's relevant and, as such, **you must eliminate all unnecessary distractions** to obtain it, like certain friends who have a penchant for overlong gabbing on the phone, etc.

---

[13] Yes, *some* measure of recreation is essential: "There's a time to weep and a time to laugh, a time to mourn and a time to dance" (Ecclesiastes 3:4).

If you don't start walking there are no steps for the Holy Spirit to guide. Think about it in terms of a guided missile: The missile cannot be guided until it's shot off. So blast off!

How exactly are you "led of the Holy Spirit" as you're walking the **path** to your **objective** according to your **plan**?

1. Be alert for "**golden opportunities**," which are **open doors** of opportunity that manifest, such as Paul's "open door," as shown in 2 Corinthians 2:12

2. Be alert for "**golden connections**," which are people who can link you to your goal one way or another.

3. "Let the **peace** of Christ rule in your heart" (Colossians 3:15) concerning every potential opportunity or connection since not every opportunity or person is from the LORD. For instance, Potiphar's wife was a connection for Joseph, but it was an ungodly connection that would've hindered him from reaching the palace (Genesis 39:6-7).

Also be conscious of proper timing: **The time for research is not the time for production or marketing**. For instance, Moses had a strong desire—a *ta'avah*—from God to deliver the Israelites from Egyptian bondage, but he acted prematurely, which caused him to be exiled to the desert for forty years (Exodus 2-3). Another good example is Joseph, who prematurely shared his vision with his jealous brothers and was subsequently sold into slavery (Genesis 37:2-28).

Say, for instance, you discern a *ta'avah* to be a full-time minister. This is great, but it's going to take years of preparation and devotion—seeking the LORD, study, consecration, mentoring, sermonizing and testing. People who jump the gun due to zeal, immaturity or impatience are bound for frustration and failure.

Throw Off Every Weight and Sin that HINDERS your Purpose

If you truly want to fulfill your God-given goal—whatever that might be—you must be willing to throw off "weights" that will burden you and sins that imprison. Notice what the Bible says on this:

> **...let us throw off <u>every thing that hinders</u> and <u>the sin that so easily entangles</u>. And let us run with perseverance the race marked out for us.**
>
> **Hebrews 12:1**

The "thing that hinders" is a "weight" that holds you down and prevents you from fulfilling your God-given objective. The thing itself is neutral and not a sin, but it saps your time and energy so much that it hinders you from completing your assignment. It could be any number of things depending on the individual—computer games, movies, golf, boating/fishing, a person, etc. These things are not necessarily evil in and of themselves, but because they distract you from your calling they are not good for you. You must either carefully guard the time you spend with such things or, if necessary, remove them from your life altogether in order to fulfill your mission.

As for the "sin that so easily entangles," this is any flesh proclivity that you've developed a taste for and it therefore seriously tempts you from time to time. You must make it a **top priority** to remove this sin from your life, whatever the cost. If you don't, it will prevent you from obtaining your God-given desire. See <u>Chapter Eleven</u> for three biblically-based keys to walking free of any sin.

The Three-Point Plan in Summary

1. Seek God first (not only) by acknowledging Him in prayer. As you do this, the Spirit will make your thoughts/desires become agreeable with His will. Longstanding desires are *ta'avahs*—earnest (righteous) desires that stay with you. The *ta'avah* is your **COURSE** (or **work, assignment, objective, mission**). It's God's will for your current (or ensuing) season in life.

2. God gave you a mind so use it. Plan your way to fulfill your God-given **COURSE** utilizing the resources at your disposal. This plan is your **WAY** (or **PATH**). At this point you have a **COURSE** and a general **WAY** to get there.

3. Now it's time for action. You will never fulfill your **COURSE** by inaction. Move toward your God-given objective based upon the plan you came up with relying on the hour-to-hour help/guidance of the Holy Spirit. This is what Proverbs means by **STEPS**—it's the Lord directing your **STEPS** along the **WAY** that you planned in order to fulfill your **COURSE**. "Let the peace of Christ reign in your heart." If you don't have a peace about something or someone be sure to bypass it/them. Be conscious of "golden connections" and "golden opportunities." It's important to start moving once you have a **COURSE** and **WAY** because if you're not walking the Lord won't be able to direct your **STEPS**.

Don't Misinterpret "the Good Life"

Someone misinterpreted elements of this teaching in one of the Fountain of Life videos and wrote me a long letter to rebuke me. He (or she) mistook my references to "the good life." I think he took it to mean living like Hugh Hefner, I don't know. However, the video itself and this chapter defines the "good life" as being hooked up with God's will and fulfilling the courses or objectives He gives you, whatever they may be. It could be moving to a third-world country and being a missionary. God's **COURSES** are exciting and good because they're in line with your Creator's will who knows you inside out and therefore how you're "wired." Yes, there will be hardships and persecutions, but He knows what you can handle and can't handle and will provide the grace to get through.

Secondly, the very beginning of both the video this chapter establishes in the plainest terms possible that I'm talking about fulfilling *righteous* desires, not unrighteous desires, like greed, hedonism and pomposity.

An Example from My Own Life

Let me share the three-point plan applied to my own life with a recent example: My 2015 book *Sheol Know* took a lot of work and discipline, particularly since it was long and detail-oriented (339 pages). To most anyone else, writing a book like this would be a mundane, arduous and tedious venture, but because writing it was based on the *ta'avah* the LORD gave me I was literally thrilled every day creating it, which isn't to say there weren't challenges, naysayers, etc.

You have to learn to **persevere** through difficulties, setbacks, ignorant criticisms, etc. in order to fulfill any significant objective God gives you, like I did with writing *Sheol Know*. As noted above, you must weed out time-wasters from your life in order to complete your course. This is vital because anything that needlessly takes your attention away from fulfilling your God-given mission isn't good and can prevent you from fulfilling your objective altogether, *if* you allow it. Also, as noted above, be on guard against any sin that can tempt you and potentially derail you, *if* you allow it. Learn to "keep with repentance" when you miss it by honestly and quickly confessing (Matthew 3:8 & Proverbs 28:13). This will keep your spiritual arteries clear of the clogging up of unconfessed sin; it will keep God's grace flowing in your life (1 Peter 5:5).

The information in this chapter is absolutely essential to anyone who wants to have a productive, meaningful life. Those who haphazardly sail thru life like a ship without a rudder will end up on the beach of despair.

Helen Keller put it best when she responded to what could be worse than blindness: "To have sight, but no vision"

Chapter Seven

Seven Keys to Spiritual Growth

In this chapter and the next one we're going to look at seven keys that guarantee spiritual growth whatever stage or level you're currently at. Here's our main text:

> **Grace and peace be yours in abundance <u>through the knowledge</u>** *(epignosis)* **<u>of God</u> and of Jesus our Lord.**
>
> **(3) His divine power has given us everything we need for life and godliness <u>through our knowledge</u>** *(epignosis)* **<u>of Him</u> who called us by his own glory and goodness. (4) Through these he has given us his very great and precious promises, so that <u>through them</u> you may <u>participate in the divine nature</u> and escape the corruption in the world caused by evil desires.**

(5) For this very reason, make every effort to add to your faith goodness; and to goodness, knowledge *(gnosis)***; (6) and to knowledge, self-control; and to self-control, perseverance; and to perseverance, godliness; (7) and to godliness, mutual affection; and to mutual affection, love. (8) For if you possess these qualities in increasing measure, they will keep you from being ineffective and unproductive in your knowledge** *(epignosis)* **of our Lord Jesus Christ. (9) But whoever does not have them is nearsighted and blind, forgetting that they have been cleansed from their past sins.**

(10) Therefore, my brothers and sisters, make every effort to confirm your calling and election. For if you do these things, you will never stumble, (11) and you will receive a rich welcome into the eternal kingdom of our Lord and Savior Jesus Christ.

2 Peter 1:2-11

This long passage contains a wealth of information absolutely vital to the effectiveness and productivity of every believer, as specified in verse 8. Let's address a few preliminary items and then examine the seven keys to spiritual growth.

Experiential Knowledge *(Epignosis)* of God

The word "knowledge" is used five times in the passage, but two different Greek words are used. In verse 5 it says that we are to add "knowledge" to our faith. This is the Greek word *gnosis (NOH-sis)*, which simply refers to the textual Word of God and the knowledge or sound doctrines thereof. This same Greek word is translated as "knowledge" in verse 6 as well. However, the other

three times "knowledge" is cited it's a different Greek word—
epignosis (ep-EE-NOH-sis)—which is simply *gnosis* with the
prefix *epi*. This isn't just textual knowledge or doctrinal
knowledge; it's *experiential* knowledge. One lexicon defines it as
"contact knowledge" or "experiential knowing" and hence
"knowledge gained through first-hand relationship."[14]

With this understanding let's look at verses 2-3 again:

> **Grace and peace be yours in abundance
> <u>through the knowledge</u>** *(epignosis)* **<u>of God</u> and of
> Jesus our Lord.**
>
> **(3) His divine power has given us
> everything we need for life and godliness
> <u>through our knowledge</u>** *(epignosis)* **<u>of Him</u> who
> called us by his own glory and goodness.**
>
> **2 Peter 1:2-3**

In both verses "knowledge"—*epignosis*—refers to the
knowledge of God and therefore to the *experiential* knowledge of
God. In other words, knowing the LORD because you've
experienced Him through applying the Word or textual knowledge,
which is *gnosis*.

The passage reveals three things we can have through
knowing God rather than just knowing *about* Him:

1. We can have "grace and peace... **in abundance**" (verse 2).
2. We can have "**everything** we need for life and godliness"
   (verse 3).
3. We can "**participate in the divine nature** and escape the
   corruption in the world caused by evil desires" (verse 4).

---

[14] HELPS Word-Studies Lexicon.

Verse 5 says that it's "for this very reason" we need to "make every effort" to add seven things to our faith, which are listed in verses 5-7: **goodness**, **knowledge** *(gnosis)*, **self-control**, **perseverance**, **godliness**, **mutual** (Christian) **affection** and **love**. The prefix "make every effort" shows that we need to be diligent about seeking and applying these seven virtues. They're not going to be automatically added to our faith and so we need to make it a **top priority**.

The context shows that we're to add them one-to-another, which helps in determining their precise meaning here. Their meaning is obvious, of course, but the context sheds light on their specific meaning in this text, as you shall see.

How to Be Productive for God and Never Fall

Verses 8-9 reveal that if we possess these seven qualities "in increasing measure" it guarantees that we'll be effective and productive (i.e. fruitful) in our walk. Those who don't have them are said to be "nearsighted and blind, forgetting that they have been cleansed from their past sins." This is talking about spiritual nearsightedness and spiritual blindness, not physical. Believers who fail to develop in these seven qualities will not be able to see afar off spiritually. In other words, they're unable to view life through the eternal lens of the Divine perspective and will thus be hampered by the limited scope of the temporal viewpoint. Moreover, they'll be spiritually *blind*. They won't be able to see the most common-sense blatant spiritual truths. In short, they'll be *dull* and constrained by the disadvantages thereof.

Another benefit of possessing these seven qualities "in increasing measure" is that it guarantees a "rich welcome" into the eternal kingdom when you come face to face with the LORD. A rich welcome is when people are excited to see you; they passionately run up to you and shake your hand, hug you or kiss you. Don't you want a welcome like this? Of course you do. Have you ever had a tepid welcome? It's no fun and it tempts you to make an about face and flee. How would you like Father God to say to the Son when you come face to face: "Oh, here comes John" with little or no enthusiasm? Thankfully, no Christian has to have such a welcome from God, but you'll have to cultivate these seven virtues to assure a rich welcome. The Word says so.

Adding the Seven Virtues to Your Faith

The seven virtues that we are to add to our faith should be viewed as *keys* to spiritual effectiveness and productivity (2 Peter 1:8). They could also be viewed as *steps* to spiritual maturity because some of them depend on the previous one to be effective. For instance, the reason you add goodness before knowledge is because only a "good and noble heart" can produce fruit when the Word is planted in it (Luke 8:15). I'll elaborate in the next couple sections.

The starting point for every believer is faith because our covenant with God is a covenant of faith. 'Covenant' means "an agreement or pact having complete terms determined by the initiating party, which are also affirmed by the one entering the agreement." A good English word for covenant is contract. All Christians have a contract with Father God through Christ by the Holy Spirit. This is the New Covenant or New Testament. Everything we receive in our agreement with the LORD is by faith because "without faith it is impossible to please God, because anyone who comes to him must believe that he exists and that he rewards those who earnestly seek him" (Hebrews 11:6).

The Bible says that every believer has a "measure of faith" otherwise they wouldn't be a believer (Romans 12:3). It's a done deal—"God has distributed" the measure of faith to everyone who's a believer. It's a gift from God (Ephesians 2:8-9) and every believer starts with the same measure.

However, it's clear from the Scriptures that **faith can grow**. For instance, Jesus noted the "little faith" of his disciples on occasion (Luke 12:28 & Matthew 14:28–31), which shows that they *could've* had more faith. In 2 Thessalonians 1:3 Paul observed that the faith of the Thessalonian believers was growing. Your faith can likewise increase, but it's dependent on YOU adding the seven qualities relayed in 2 Peter 1:5-7—**goodness, knowledge, self-control, perseverance, godliness, mutual** (Christian) **affection** and **love**.

You'll note that there are *seven* virtues. This is fitting since the number 7 is identified with something being "finished" or "complete" in the Bible. Thus, if you are diligent to add these seven qualities to your walk *you* will be complete as a man or woman of God. Praise the Lord!

Let's now look at each one.

Adding Goodness (Virtue)

I'm probably going to spend a little more time on this first key than the other six. You'll see why.

First, let's review the applicable verse from our main text:

> **make every effort to add to your faith goodness; and to goodness, knowledge;**
> **2 Peter 1:5**

"Goodness" is translated from the Greek word *arête (ar-ET-ay)*, which means "moral excellence," "uprightness" or "good quality" and is translated as "virtue" in the King James Version. The same Greek word is used to describe the LORD in verse 3 of the text and, as such, God is of superior moral excellence and uprightness.

Note that goodness must be added *before* knowledge. As pointed out earlier, "knowledge" here is *gnosis* in the Greek and therefore refers to textual knowledge. Why add moral excellence before knowledge? Simply because it prepares the soil of your heart for the seed of the Word of God. You see, **the quality of the soil of your heart determines the productiveness of God's Word in your life**. If your heart is of bad quality the Word will produce little or no results; if it is of mediocre quality, it will only produce okay results. However, if it is of good, moral quality it will produce *good* results!

For proof of this, let's look at…

The Parable of the Sower

Luke 8:4-8 relays the story of a farmer scattering seed that lands on four types of soil: **1.** The **hardened soil** of a path where the seeds were trampled by people, and then birds came and ate them; **2.** the **rocky ground** where the plants started to grow, but withered because there wasn't enough water; **3.** the **thorny soil** where the plants started to sprout, but were choked by the thorns; and **4.** the good soil, which yielded a huge crop. We don't have to wonder what this parable means because Jesus explained it:

> **This is the meaning of the parable: The seed is the word of God. (12) Those along the path are the ones who hear, and then the devil comes and takes away the word from their hearts, so that they may not believe and be saved. (13) Those on the rocky ground are the ones who receive the word with joy when they hear it, but they have no root. They believe for a while, but in the time of testing they fall away. (14) The seed that fell among thorns stands for those who hear, but as they go on their way they are choked by life's worries, riches and pleasures, and they do not mature. (15) But the**

seed on <u>good soil</u> stands for those with <u>a noble</u> <u>and good heart, who hear the word, retain it,</u> <u>and by persevering produce a crop.</u>

Luke 8:11-15

The "seed" that's scattered on the four soils is the Word of God. Notice that Jesus didn't specify what element of God's Word the seed represents, like the gospel message. That's because the seed refers to the Word of God in general. It refers to any truth contained in God's Word that can bless you or save you.

The four types of soil represent the quality of four types of hearts. Observe the results of each type of soil:

1. **The Hardened Soil:** The seeds could not take root at all in the hardened soil of the path and birds came and ate them. Some people's hearts are so hard for one reason or another that the Word of God can't even take root. So Satan is able to immediately steal the Word.

2. **The Rocky Soil:** The seeds could not take root in the rocky soil because there wasn't enough moisture; that is, water. God's Word is likened to water in the Bible (Ephesians 5:26) because it feeds our faith on any given truth. When there's not enough water faith withers and dies.

3. **The Thorny Soil:** The seeds that fell in the thorny soil started to sprout but were choked by the thorns, which represent life's worries, riches (the love of money) and various pleasures. The rocky soil and the thorny soil show that there are four things that will prevent the Word of God from bearing fruit in our lives: (1.) Lack of the watering of the Word, which feeds faith, (2.) the anxieties of life, (3.) preoccupation with money/wealth and (4.) various pleasures—good or bad—that preoccupy one's time.

4. **The Good Soil:** The Word of God can only produce fruit from "the good and noble heart" (verse 15).

I trust you see why it's necessary to add goodness *before* the knowledge of God's Word.

How Do You Add Goodness?

Adding goodness is a simple matter once you understand the nature of your mind & heart and the fact that each person is the "guardian" of his/her soul. To explain, let's turn to a powerful passage that conveys a vital principle that, believe it or not, determines the very course of your life:

> **Above all else, <u>guard your heart</u>, for it is the wellspring of life.**
>
> **Proverbs 4:23**

When a passage prefaces what it says with "above all else" it means that what it's about to say is of the utmost importance. So this verse is saying that **guarding your heart needs to be a top priority in your life**.

Your heart is the **core of your mind** and things get rooted in your heart based on your **thought life** and **the ideas, desires or fears you choose to meditate on**, that is, **feed.** This explains why the New Century Version of the Bible —a paraphrase—translates the verse like so:

> **Be careful what you think, <u>because your thoughts run your life</u>.**
>
> **Proverbs 4:23** (NCV)

Be careful what you choose to think about—impulses, images, inclinations, worries, desires, fears, etc.—because *what you decide to dwell on in your mind will run your very life!*

Notice again how the NIV puts it: Guard your heart for it is the **wellspring** of life. The word "wellspring" in the Hebrew is *totsa'ah* (rhymes with matzah ball), which means "source" or "geographical boundaries." In other words, whatever you allow to occupy your heart—your thought life—becomes the source of your very life and **determines your geographical boundaries**; that is, *how far you go or how far you don't go*. Put differently, what you allow to get rooted in your heart determines what you will be!

This corresponds to what Jesus said: "A good man brings good things out of the good stored up in his heart, and an evil man brings evil things out of the evil stored up in his heart" (Luke 6:45). People produce according to what's in their heart. This is why the Bible likens the human heart to soil, as shown in the aforementioned Parable of the Sower (Luke 8:4-15). Just as soil is neutral and grows whatever is planted in it—whether quality produce or weeds & thornbushes—so the heart is neutral and grows whatever you allow to get rooted in it, whether good or bad, productive or destruction, beautiful or hideous, pure or profane.

You must understand that you have two conflicting natures: a godly nature, which is your spirit, and a sinful nature, which is your flesh. This explains something Jesus said: "Watch and pray so that you will not fall into temptation. The **spirit** is willing, but the **flesh** is weak" (Matthew 26:41). Because your spirit is your godly nature it wants to do what is right, but because your flesh is your sinful nature it wants to do what is wrong. Your higher nature *wants* to do what is positive, productive and righteous whereas your lower nature wants to do what is negative, destructive and unrighteous. These two natures are in conflict with each other and are constantly sending images and impulses to your mind (Galatians 5:17). Whichever ones you accept and feed will get lodged in your heart. This explains Paul's instructions to meditate on positive things in Philippians 4:8 because **whatever you meditate on inhabits your thought life and will get lodged in your heart**. The more you feed it the more it'll grow. You'll thus **produce accordingly**.

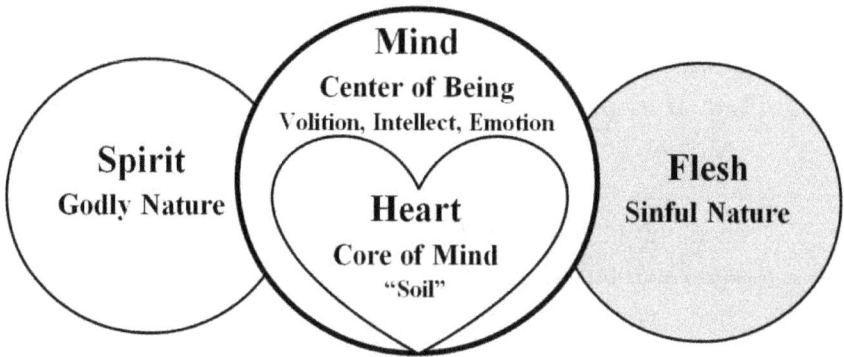

God works with you through your spirit—your godly nature—by the Holy Spirit whereas demonic spirits work with you through your flesh—the sinful nature. These two natures are **in conflict** and the one you heed will determine if you're spirit-controlled or flesh-ruled. If you're spirit-controlled you'll produce the fruit of the spirit whereas if you're flesh-ruled you'll produce works of the flesh (Galatians 5:17-23). It's your **choice** because, whether you know it or not, you possess the **power of volition**; that is, the **power of decision**.

Let me give an example of something negative getting lodged in a person's heart: A pedophile in prison wrote Ann Landers years ago. He confessed that he was a pedophile and that his time in prison had not set him free—the walls could not change him. There was this "monster" in his heart, he said, and when he would be released in 7 months he was going to continue to do the very monstrous things that got him sent to prison in the first place. Why? Because he was in *bondage* to this evil desire that was lodged in his heart. In other words, **this wicked desire that he allowed to get rooted in his heart by occupying his thought life was literally determining the course of his life!** The good news is that there's hope for people like this if they're willing to humbly turn to the LORD in repentance & faith and put into practice the wisdom of God's Word (e.g. Isaiah 55:6-9).

So you "add" goodness by:

1. Actively meditating on good things—images, impulses, desires—which automatically push out the bad. This is the **law of displacement**: Two things cannot occupy the same space at the same time. You can't walk in faith and fear simultaneously; you're walking in one or the other. By choosing to focus on faith you weed out fear. Needless to say, weed out the negative things from your heart!

2. Guard your heart from negative things. In other words, be proactive as **the guardian of your soul**. Don't allow bad things to occupy your thought life because the corresponding desire will manifest as you dwell on them. And the more you meditate on them the more the desire grows. For instance, if you dwell on negative, hopeless thoughts it'll give birth to depression, meaninglessness, frustration and, if it's bad enough, suicide. Another example: If there's a married person at work who starts flirting with you and you're tempted to think about her or him in unwholesome ways, don't allow such thoughts to get rooted in your thought life. If you do they'll give birth to desire and desire ultimately gives birth to action (James 1:14-15).

Since things get planted in your heart through **1.** what you see, **2.** what you hear and **3.** the company you keep or the atmosphere you permit, it's important to discipline what you allow your eyes to see, your ears to hear and the people with whom you spend time.

You can look at adding goodness as removing the "dross" from your life so the LORD can forge a worthy vessel for His purposes. This coincides with Proverbs 25:4: "Remove the dross from the silver and out comes material for the silversmith." Dross is waste material that a metallurgist removes in order to forge the quality instrument of his choice. It's the same thing with God and you. Here's a harmonizing New Testament passage:

> **In a large house there are articles not only
> of gold and silver, but also of wood and clay;
> some are for <u>noble</u> purposes and some for
> <u>ignoble</u>. (21) Those who <u>cleanse themselves</u> from
> the latter will be instruments for <u>noble</u> purposes,
> made holy, useful to the Master and prepared to
> do any good work.**
>
> 2 Timothy 2:20-21

So be sure to weed out the dross in your life and, above all else: **Be careful what you think because your thoughts run your life!** By doing this you're "adding" goodness to your faith.

Adding Knowledge to Goodness

Verse 5 of our text says that we are to add knowledge to goodness. As already noted "knowledge" in the Greek is *gnosis (NOH-sis)*, which means textual knowledge or sound doctrine.

In order to add knowledge you must make the decision to feed on God's Word and cultivate passion, as David did:

> **I have <u>chosen</u> the way of <u>truth</u>;**
> **I have set my heart on <u>your laws</u>.**
>
> **Psalm 119:30**

David *decided* to live according God's truth and so he set his heart on God's law, which is a reference to the revealed Word of God at the time.

> **My soul is consumed with longing**
> **for your laws at all times.**
>
> **Psalm 119:20**

Note David's palpable passion! No wonder he's referred to in both the Old and New Testaments as "a man after God's own heart." I encourage you to develop the same passion for God's Word.

The best way to tackle this topic is to simply throw out numerous points to keep in mind in your pursuit of knowledge:

- YOU have an anointing to receive from the Word **yourself**, by the Holy Spirit (1 John 2:27). Feed on it yourself!

- Always remember the four basic laws of hermeneutics, which we looked at in <u>Chapter Three</u>, but they bear repeating:
  - ➤ **Context is king:** Meaning the surrounding text reveals the obvious meaning of each passage
  - ➤ **Scripture interprets Scripture:** Meaning every passage must be interpreted in light of the context of the entire Bible and that the Bible itself is its best interpreter. In other words, one's interpretation of a passage must gel with what the rest of Scripture teaches; the more overt and detailed passages obviously expand our understanding of the more sketchy and ambiguous ones.
  - ➤ **Take the Bible literally unless it's clear that figurative language is being used:** In which case you look for the literal truth that the symbolism intends to convey.
  - ➤ **If the plain sense makes sense—and is in harmony with the rest of Scripture—don't look for any other sense lest you end up with nonsense:** This includes the "plain sense" of the whole of Scripture on any given topic. In other words, if an individual or group comes up with an interpretation that is opposed to the plain-sense meaning that all the passages in the Bible

obviously point to on that subject then it must be rejected. You may have noticed that this fourth rule is essentially the other three combined.

- Develop a reading plan as you're more apt to stick with something if you have a plan (Proverbs 16:1 & 9).
  - ➤ A good plan that works for me is to split the Bible up into sections and read 1 or 2 chapters from each section. The sections are: Gospels & Acts, Epistles, Psalms, Proverbs, the Law (or Torah) and the Prophetic books.
  - ➤ Change translations from time to time. Everyone has a favorite translation, but periodically reading other translations keeps things fresh as it provides the opportunity to read the same text in a different light.
  - ➤ A thousand mile journey begins with one step.
  - ➤ "Feed" from the Scriptures via hearing, reading, memorizing, studying and meditating (Matthew 4:4):

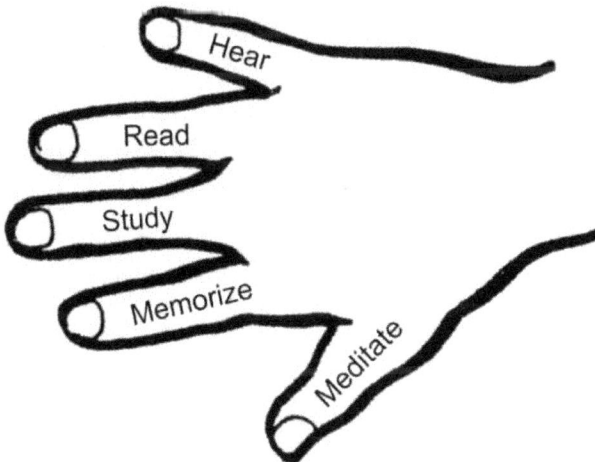

Notice that the thumb refers to meditation, which shows that you hear the Word *and* meditate; read the Word *and* Meditate; study the Word *and* meditate; and memorize the Word *and* meditate.

➢ Growth in the Scriptures is like taking a helicopter ride—you see more and more the further you go up.

- Consider topical studies from time to time. What subject interests you?
  ➢ Endeavor to master that subject.
  ➢ What's the **Bible itself** say on the subject? Religious tradition isn't always right. Sometimes it's downright false.
  ➢ Research what others have to say via books, websites, audio teachings, videos, etc.

- The proof of desire is pursuit (Proverbs 2:1-6). If you want knowledge, understanding and wisdom you have to earnestly **pursue it!**

- If your Bible reading time seems dry and you're not getting much out of it, get into the habit of sincerely *praying* for understanding before you read. After all, Jesus said "Ask and it will be given to you; seek and you will find; knock and the door will be opened to you" (Matthew 7:7). This explains why Paul prayed for believers in this manner: "we have not stopped praying for you and asking God to fill you with the knowledge of his will through all spiritual wisdom and understanding" (Colossians 1:9). This also explains this powerful passage from the biblical book of wisdom:

if you <u>call out for insight</u> and <u>cry aloud for understanding</u>, (4) and <u>if</u> you <u>look for it</u> as for silver and <u>search for it</u> as for hidden treasure, (5) <u>then</u> you will understand the fear of the LORD and find the knowledge of God. (6)

For the LORD gives wisdom, and from his mouth come knowledge and understanding.

Proverbs 2:3-6

> ➤ The passage encourages us to passionately seek insight and understanding by crying out for it and calling aloud. God blesses such diligent pursuit because "He rewards those who earnestly seek him" (Hebrews 11:6). It's an axiom.

> ➤ After praying for knowledge, understanding and wisdom. *Expect* to learn and be blessed.

- Make sure a revelation is true and 'works' before proclaiming it. Don't jump the gun; be patient. As an example, I first discovered the truths conveyed in *Sheol Know* back in 1996 and waited *twelve years* before going public with the information!

> ➤ The Bible says the mind needs to be renewed (Romans 12:1-2) and is therefore perfectly capable of coming up with all kinds of erroneous "insights." Also consider the fact that the Bible acknowledges the teachings of demons (1 Timothy 4:1), which suggests that whoever teaches or embraces these teachings received insight or "revelation" from demonic spirits, who are *lying* spirits. Revelation that's accurate, by contrast, comes from the Holy Spirit, who guides us "into all **truth**" (John 16:13). The Holy Spirit is called the "Spirit of truth" (John 16:13); consequently, whatever revelation you get from the Spirit of truth will gel with the "word of truth" (2 Timothy 2:15), meaning it will conform to sound **hermeneutics**; that is, the aforementioned four principle rules of bible interpretation.

- Apprehend quality mentors near and far. A mentor is simply someone who positively influences you through knowledge, example or motivation.
  - ➤ Realize that you can only go so far by yourself (Acts 8:30-31). Don't be an unteachable, stubborn fool.
  - ➤ "Feed" from those who minister the Word locally (via church services, etc.) and long-distance (via websites, books, videos, radio, etc.). The primary purpose of the fivefold ministry gifts—apostle, prophet, evangelist, pastor and teacher—is prayer and *the ministry (i.e. serving) of the Word* (Ephesians 4:11-13, Acts 6:1-4 & 1 Timothy 5:17).
  - ➤ The ministry of the Word prompts spiritual growth and enables you to reach your maximum potential in Christ.
  - ➤ One of the main reasons believers fail to reach their maximum potential is because they cut themselves off from the ministry of the Word (Proverbs 19:27).
  - ➤ Learn from mentors but don't worship mentors; that is, don't make the mistake of viewing them as infallible in doctrine and practice because you *will* be let down.
  - ➤ Flee from unworthy "mentors" who are arrogant and abusive, utilizing methods like bluster, intimidation and unnecessary insults.
  - ➤ Realize that those who transfer knowledge can also transfer error. So "eat the meat and spit out the bones."
  - ➤ Don't limit yourself to the limitations of a mentor. Just because they've limited themselves doesn't mean you have to do the same.
  - ➤ If you are diligent you'll likely pass up your mentors, as David did (Psalm 119:99-100).

- Develop the all-your-heart ethic; don't settle for okay or good—strive to be exceptional! (Ecclesiastes 9:10 & Colossians 3:23).

- Persevere through spiritual growth pangs.

- Be aware of hindrances to growth and shun them like the plague, such as:
  - ➤ **Pride**—an "I know it all" attitude or superiority complex.
  - ➤ **Erroneous religious tradition**—false beliefs that have passed on for centuries are difficult to escape. *Escape!*
  - ➤ **Rigid sectarianism**, which is addressed at length in <u>Chapter Three</u> (Luke 9:49-50 & 1 Corinthians 1:12-13).
  - ➤ **Closed-mindedness**. Endeavor to cultivate the "Berean spirit," like the Bereans who were excited about Paul's teaching, which deviated from the Berean's set doctrine and the limitations thereof (Acts 17:11).

Adding Self-Control to Knowledge

Verse 6 of our text (2 Peter 1) says we're to add self-control to knowledge. 'Self-control' in the Greek is *egkrateia (eng-KRAT-ee-ah)*, which means self-mastery, self-restraint or dominion within. It's self-control proceeding out of oneself, but not necessarily by oneself. Since we're to add self-control *to* knowledge it contextually means we're to **control ourselves according to the knowledge we received**. In other words, we're to **put into practice God's Word after we receive it**. That's all it means.

The reason adding this quality is vital is obvious: What good is knowing God's Word if you don't actually practice it? Doing so is foolish and Jesus addressed it in this passage (which we previously looked at in <u>Chapter Three</u>):

> **"Therefore everyone who <u>hears these words of mine and puts them into practice</u> is like a wise man who built his house on the rock. (25) The rain came down, the streams rose, and the winds blew and beat against that house; yet it did not fall, because it had its foundation on the rock. (26) But everyone who <u>hears these words of mine and does not put them into practice</u> is like a foolish man who built his house on sand. (27) The rain came down, the streams rose, and the winds blew and beat against that house, and it fell with a great crash."**
>
> **Matthew 7:24-27**

The Lord is talking about two kinds of people who hear the Word of God. One is wise because he puts it into practice whereas the other is foolish because he *doesn't* put it into practice. In both cases Jesus says the "rain came down, the streams rose, and the winds blew." This refers to attacks from the kingdom of darkness "for the Word's sake" (KJV). If you don't know what I'm talking about, earlier this chapter we saw in the Parable of the Sower that those who receive God's Word will undergo a "time of testing" (Luke 8:13). Mark's account puts it like this: "trouble or persecution *come* **because of the word**" (Mark 4:17). Whenever someone receives the Word the enemy will come and try to steal it via some kind of attack. The wise person who puts into practice God's Word will withstand the attack whereas the foolish person who fails to put it into practice will not. The latter person is apt to conclude that "God's Word doesn't work" when it has nothing to do with the truthfulness of the Word of God or the faithfulness of the Lord.

So "build your house on the rock" by simply putting into practice God's Word. If it says "husbands love your wives" then love your wife if you're a husband (Ephesians 5:25). If it says "slander no one" then be sure to slander no one, which includes gossip since gossip typically devolves into slander (Titus 3:2). Whatever the Word of God instructs you to do—as long as it's relevant to the New Testament believer[15]—put it into practice. In short, DO IT. If your life is messed up due to the flesh or adhering to false beliefs, practicing "the word of truth" is the remedy (2 Timothy 2:15); it'll turn your ship around, so to speak, just give it time.

Practicing Positional Truth

As important as it is to practice *practical* truth it's just as important to practice *positional* truth. A "positional truth" is any truth from Scripture that reveals how God sees you in covenant with Him, which is your *position*. For the New Testament believer, meaning YOU, this is **who you are** in your spirit, the "new self" (Ephesians 4:22-24). Who are you in your spirit?

1. You are **holy** (Colossians 1:21-22).
2. You are a **child of God** (John 1:12-13).
3. You are a **new creation** (2 Corinthians 5:17).
4. You are the **righteousness of God** (2 Corinthians 5:21).
5. You are **dead to sin** (Romans 6:11,14,18).
6. You are **more than a conqueror** (Romans 8:37).
7. You are a **temple of the Holy Spirit** (1 Corinthians 6:19-20).
8. You are **rich** (2 Corinthians 8:9).
9. You are **healed** (1 Peter 2:24).
10. You are a **royal priest** or **priestess** of the Most High God (1 Peter 2:9)!

---

[15] In other words, don't practice anything that's *strictly* applicable to someone else of a different era and covenant, like the Israelites under Old Testament law who offered animal sacrifices to cover their sins; Jesus took care of all that in the new covenant so believers don't have to concern themselves with it.

How do you practice positional truths? You practice them simply by believing them and not disagreeing with them. Remember, **"The tongue has the power of life and death"** so utilize this power accordingly (Proverbs 18:21). Never speak words that contradict who God says you are. **Never!** This is tantamount to calling God a liar. Be sure to chew on these amazing positional truths and others as well. Make them your **meditation** and your **confession.** Take David, for example. He was diligent to "meditate" on God's Word, as shown in Psalm 119:15-16. The Hebrew word for 'meditate' is *siyach (SEE-ahk),* which means "to ponder and converse with oneself and, hence, out loud" (Strong 115). As you do this, you'll grow in understanding and power. The more these truths become a part of you the more you'll be set free of the flesh and the more you'll **soar in the spirit** FREE of the limitations of the mental plane.[16]

Again, Jesus said we must "continue" in his word if we are to "know the truth" and be set "free." Growing in knowledge, understanding and wisdom on *a continuing basis* is the key to this.

The Power of the Tongue

Speaking of the power of words, Proverbs 4:24 says to "keep corrupt talk far from your lips." The root Hebrew word for 'corrupt' is *luz (looz),* which means "to turn aside or depart from what is right or good." To practice this Scripture you must realize the power of your tongue:

> **The tongue has the power of <u>life and death</u>, and those who love it will eat its fruit.**
> **Proverbs 18:21**

---

[16] For important details on this topic see the video "How God Sees YOU" at the Fountain of Life website or youtube.

The "fruit" of the tongue is good, but only "those who love it will eat its fruit." This means only those who realize and value the tongue's power.

You must get a hold of the fact that your tongue is a powerful gift from God, which has the potential to bless or destroy. Only those who realize the value of the tongue will experience **the fruit** it has to offer.

Exactly how powerful is the tongue? The Bible likens it to the small rudder of a large ship that steers the vessel wherever the pilot wants it to go (James 3:2-6). Think about it: The **very course of your life** is linked to what you do with your tongue. How so?

Your words are **creative forces** or **destructive forces**. Let's look at **examples** of both.

- Words have **THE POWER OF LIFE**:
  - ➤ The earth & universe were **created** at God's command (Hebrews 11:3). You were created in God's likeness and therefore your words have creative power as well.
  - ➤ God promised Abram countless offspring (Genesis 15:5), but Abram was still childless 24 years later at the age of 91.
    - o God changed his name to Abraham, which means "father of a multitude" (17:3-5).
    - o Abraham and everyone else were in essence forced by God to speak of Abraham as "father of a multitude." And so the promise came to pass (Romans 4:18).
  - ➤ The priestly blessing *blessed* people: "The LORD bless you and keep you; the LORD make his face shine on you and be gracious to you; the LORD turn his face toward you and give you peace" (Numbers 6:22-27).
    - o To 'bless' means "to speak positive words that have a productive impact."
  - ➤ Jesus **blessed** the children (Mark 10:13,16).

> Your words, combined with belief, can remove obstacles (Mark 11:22-23).

- Words have **THE POWER OF DEATH**:
  - To 'curse' means "to speak negative words that have a destructive impact." The Bible likens the tongue to a sword that can harm people (Proverbs 12:18 & Psalm 64:3).
> An influential person tells a little girl she's "fat," which she takes to heart and becomes anorexic.
> Parents curse their very own children; the kids take the evil words to heart and the words essentially become a deadly prophecy in their lives.
  - Thankfully, underserved curses have no power over you, **unless you allow it** (Proverbs 26:2): "an undeserved curse does not come to rest."
  - Counteract curses by speaking blesses over yourself. For instance, you can take 1 Peter 2:9 and say: "**I** am a part of a **chosen people**, a **royal priesthood**, a **holy nation**, **God's special possession**, that I may declare the praises of Him who called me out of darkness into his wonderful light." Speak it with fervor!
> People speak curses *over themselves*: e.g. "I'm so clumsy," "I always get sick during flu season," "I *can't* do it"—"*I can't,*" "*I can't,*" "*I can't,*" "*I can't.*" Because they speak it and start believing it the words come to pass.
  - **Never** speak ill of yourself, your worth, your work or your goals. If you do, you're cursing your own life, which could become a self-fulfilling prophecy.
  - **If you say anything enough you'll eventually believe it**; and as a person thinks or believes in their

heart, so they are (Proverbs 23:7 KJV, Proverbs 27:19 & Matthew 12:34-35).

- o Your words **advertise** who you are and **where you are going**, like **signposts**.
- o Reject the **victim vocabulary**—"I was abused" or "I don't have an education."

➤ We are to bless others (Romans 12:14), but *sometimes* cursing is in order, like when Jesus **cursed** the fig tree (Mark 11:12-14, 20-21) or when Paul cursed Elymas (*el-OO-mass*) (Acts 13:8-12).

Here's one last powerful passage on the subject to chew on:

From the fruit of their lips people are filled with good things, as surely as the works of their hands reward them.

Proverbs 12:14

Needless to say, "add self-control" to knowledge by lining up your actions and tongue (words) with the Word. Amen.

Adding Perseverance to Self-Control

Verse 6 of our text (2 Peter 1) says that we are to add perseverance to self-control. 'Perseverance' in the Greek is *hupomoné (hoop-om-on-AY)*, which means endurance, steadfastness or to wait patiently. So after preparing the soil of your heart to insure that it's good soil and then adding the Word and putting it into practice, **it's *then* necessary to add perseverance for the Word to produce fruit in your life**.

Let me give an example: several years ago I had an irritating skin rash on the back of my hand for over two years. I showed it to my doctor during a check-up and he referred me to a dermatologist. I had no desire to waste time or money on a skin doctor so I continued to put up with the rash until I got righteously angry over it one night. The Spirit strongly impressed me to curse the rash from the roots repeatedly and speak healing over the back of my hand until it was gone and that's exactly what I did. I cursed the rash, commanded it to die and leave my body; and then blessed my hand, loosing healing and health. Guess what happened? The rash completely disappeared, but it took a while—nine weeks, in fact— and I had to be stubbornly tenacious, especially when it would reoccur after starting to die out. This is perseverance or following through. **Faith and the Word of God are not enough in such cases; you must add perseverance, which is patience**. The Bible emphasizes that it's through faith and patience that we inherit what is promised, not just faith:

> **We do not want you to become lazy, but to imitate those who <u>through faith and patience</u> inherit what has been promised.**
> **Hebrews 6:12**

I said above that it took nine weeks for the healing to manifest. What if I *gave up* on week 8? The healing wouldn't have manifested. This shows that you have to persevere when you practice the Word in order for it to produce lasting fruit.

Now consider adding perseverance to something else entirely, like your pursuit of truth and all that goes with it; i.e. acquiring knowledge, understanding and wisdom. Notice what Jesus said:

> **"If you <u>continue</u> in my word, you are truly my disciples; and you will know the truth, and the truth will make you free"**
> **John 8:31-32** (NRSV)

The Christ said that only those who *continue* in His Word—persevere in it—will know the truth, not those who give up after a season of seeking and studying. He also didn't say that those who conveniently and lazily embrace the official doctrines of this or that sect will know the truth. No, only those who *continue* in God's Word will know the truth; and the more you continue—honestly seek and study—the more knowledge, understanding and insight you'll have. Persevere in God's Word and don't give up!

Chapter Eight

Seven Keys to Spiritual Growth Part 2

Applying the first four keys to your faith—goodness, knowledge, self-control and perseverance—will result in fruit in your life. In other words, these four keys guarantee the fruitfulness of God's Word. They each concern the planting, cultivation and fruit-bearing of the Word.

The last three keys, by contrast, involve **walking in love** in our **relationships**, starting with the LORD ("godliness"), then fellow believers ("mutual affection") and, lastly, people in the world ("love"). The reason this is important is revealed in this passage:

> **For in Christ Jesus neither circumcision nor uncircumcision means anything, but <u>faith working through love</u>.**
>
> **Galatians 5:6** (NASB)

Our covenant with God is a covenant of faith and therefore it works through faith; and faith **works** *through* **love**. If you cancel out love you cancel out faith and your covenant won't "work" as it should.

With this understanding, let's freshen up on our main text and then consider the fifth key, which is godliness:

> **His divine power has given us everything we need for life and <u>godliness</u> through our knowledge of him who called us by his own glory and goodness. (4) Through these he has given us his very great and precious promises, so that through them you may participate in the divine nature, having escaped the corruption in the world caused by evil desires.**
>
> **(5) For this very reason, make every effort to add to your faith goodness; and to goodness, knowledge; (6) and to knowledge, self-control; and to self-control, perseverance; and to perseverance, <u>godliness</u>; (7) and to godliness, <u>mutual affection</u>; and to mutual affection, <u>love</u>. (8) For if you possess these qualities in increasing measure, they will keep you from being ineffective and unproductive in your knowledge of our Lord Jesus Christ. (9) But whoever does not have them is nearsighted and blind, forgetting that they have been cleansed from their past sins.**
>
> **2 Peter 1:3-9**

Adding Godliness

The Greek for "Godliness" in the Bible is not the same as the Greek for "religion." The former is *eusebeia (yoo-SEB-ee-ah)* whereas the latter is *thréskeia (thrays-KIH-ah)*. Notice how the Greek scholar E.W. Bullinger distinguishes the two words:

> *Eusebeia* [godliness] relates to a real, true, vital, and spiritual relation with God while *thréskeia* [religion] relates to the outward acts of religious observances or ceremonies, which can be done in the flesh. Our English word "religion" was never used in the sense of true godliness. It always meant the outward forms of worship (Bullinger 335).

So **godliness refers to genuine spiritual relationship with the LORD** as opposed to religion, which refers to outward religious acts. Godliness *cannot* be performed by the flesh whereas religion can.

Godliness could simply be translated as "like-God-ness." In other words, it's behaving and speaking as the Lord would behave and speak. You could say it's *imitating* God, which we are plainly instructed to do in the Bible (Ephesians 5:1 & 1 Peter 4:11). There are two ways to do this. One is to find out what the Word of God instructs and simply put it into practice. Since this is *already covered* in verses 5-6 of our main text—i.e. adding self-control to knowledge—this is not what verse 6 is talking about when it says we're to add godliness. No, godliness in this context refers to loving God in a different way than obeying His Word (1 John 5:3); it's referring to loving Him in a relational sense.

How would this make a person godly; that is, *like*-God? Simple: The more time you spend with a person, particularly someone you love and respect, the closer you'll become and the more *like* him or her you'll naturally be. It's the same thing with your relationship with God. The more time you spend with Him, the closer you'll become and the more *like* Him you'll be. The LORD will "rub off" on you and you'll thus be increasingly *like*-God or godly.

With the understanding of what godliness is, we are encouraged to *pursue* it in the Bible:

> **For the love of money is a root of all kinds of evil. Some people, eager for money, have wandered from the faith and pierced themselves with many griefs.**
> **(11) But flee from these things, you man of God, and <u>pursue</u> righteousness, <u>godliness</u>, faith, love, perseverance [and] gentleness**
> **1 Timothy 6:10-11**

We're also encouraged to *train* ourselves to be godly:

> **Have nothing to do with godless myths and old wives' tales; rather, <u>train yourself to be godly</u>. (8) For physical training is of some value, but <u>godliness</u> has value for all things, holding promise for both the present life and the life to come.**
> **1 Timothy 4:7-8**

(NOTE: Both "godly" in verse 7 and "godliness" in verse 8 are the same Greek word, the aforementioned *eusebeia*).

I'm citing these two passages to stress that godliness—which is an active and increasingly intimate relationship with the LORD—won't automatically happen; it must be pursued and you have to "train yourself" to habitually walk in it. This is understandable when you consider that **all good relationships take time, energy, attention and discipline**. It's no different with your relationship with God.

For important details about godliness in the sense of communing with the LORD see the last four sections of <u>Chapter Four</u>.

Godliness Vs. Religion

As noted above, godliness and religion are altogether different. Godliness refers to an active relationship with God and the corresponding "rubbing off" effect where you become increasingly like-God whereas religion relates to outward acts of service and devotion. Religion in this sense is good as long as the person balances it out with godliness. However, religion without godliness devolves into sterile go-through-the-motions religiosity.

If you've read the last four sections of Chapter Four then you know godliness involves both simple communion with the Lord and praise & worship. I have to be careful how I word this because I don't want to be taken the wrong way, so please read with discernment:

Of course it's better to enter into praise & worship once or twice a week in the assembly of the saints than not at all, that's a given. But celebration and adoration of God should become more of an everyday thing as the believer grows. Praise & worship should flow out of us as naturally as water from a spring (Hebrews 13:15). This is the way it should be for growing believers and more seasoned ones alike. But something's seriously wrong if praising and worshipping God becomes mere outward antics at church services. When this happens, the believer is essentially just putting on an act because he or she is around other believers, but it's not a reality in his/her personal life. Beware of falling into this mode because it's a form of legalism—counterfeit "Christianity"—which Jesus denounced when he quoted Isaiah:

> **"These people honor me with their lips,**
> **but their hearts are far from me."**
>
> **Mark 7:6**

It's possible to praise & worship God with our mouths and yet not really mean it with our hearts. Please be careful to never slip into such a legalistic mode!

Believe it or not, churches sometimes unknowingly facilitate this problem. They put so much stress on coming to every church service and being involved in the church that believers end up running around like headless chickens doing this or that for the ministry, which leaves very little time for the most important thing, their *relationship* with God. This is especially so when you factor in other life essentials like work, kids, education, shopping, cooking, physical fitness, rest and recreation.[17] In other words, believers are so pressured to run around doing this or that so their pastors will deem them faithful and godly that they don't have time and energy for the very things that create true godliness—personal time spent with the LORD and his Word.

This could just as easily happen to pastors and worship leaders or musicians. Such people become so involved in the work of the ministry that they forsake the core of all Christian service, the Lord himself. The story of Mary and Martha applies here:

> **As Jesus and the disciples were on their way, he came to a village where a woman named Martha opened her home to him. (39) She had a sister called <u>Mary, who sat at the Lord's feet listening to what he said</u>. (40) But <u>Martha was distracted by all the preparations</u> that had to be made. She came to him and asked, "Lord, don't you care that my sister has left me to do <u>the work</u> by myself? <u>Tell her to help me!</u>"**
>
> **(41) "Martha, Martha," the Lord answered, "you are worried and upset about**

---

[17] Yes, *some* measure of recreation is essential: "There's a time to weep and a time to laugh, a time to mourn and a time to dance" (Ecclesiastes 3:4).

many things, (42) but <u>only one thing is needed</u>, Mary has chosen <u>what is better</u> and it will not be taken away from her."

Luke 10:38-42

Martha was so focused on the busy-ness of *working* for the Lord that she unintentionally forsook what was most important—spending time with him and "listening to what he said," an obvious reference to spending quality time with the LORD personally and His Word. In fact, Martha was so involved with the work of her service—her *ministry*—that she got mad at someone else who was free of such concerns and spending personal time with the Lord. So mad, in fact, that she started demanding things from the very One she was supposed to be serving! She TOLD the Lord, "Tell her to help me!" This is what religion without godliness does to people: It corrupts them to the point that they end up having the very *opposite* attitude they should have.

Serving God is a wonderful thing, but don't be foolish like Martha and get your priorities out of whack. Think about it, the Living Lord was AT HER HOUSE—the amazing miracle-worker—and all she does is run around in a whirlwind of activity? Mary chose what was more important on this occasion and Jesus even commends her for it. There's a time for doing works of service for the Lord, of course, but there's also a time for your relationship. The latter's more important because **our service for the Lord must spring *from* our love for Him**. Otherwise it's just religious works or, worse, putting on a show.

E.W. Bullinger noted above that godliness in the sense of communion with the Lord and worship cannot be performed by the flesh, whereas religious acts can. The flesh gets uncomfortable during praise & worship or intimate prayer. It can't handle godliness, but it's perfectly fine performing religious works, including going to church, taking notes, etc. Not that there's anything wrong with these activities, as long as they're balanced out by godliness. The flesh is comfortable working for the Lord or doing things in the name of being devotional rather than spending relational time with Him, which was the case with Martha.

Adding Mutual (Christian) Affection and Love

As noted at the beginning of this chapter, the last three virtues we're instructed to add to our faith in 2 Peter 1:5-7 have to do with **walking in love in our relationships**. "Godliness" has to do with loving God in a vital relationship whereas the next two virtues—"mutual affection" and "love"—have to do with loving **1.** fellow believers and **2.** people in the world.

These last two qualities stem from two well-known Greek words for love. The Greek for "Mutual affection" is often translated as "brotherly kindness" in other English versions and that's how the original NIV renders it. The revised NIV obviously changed it to "mutual affection" to make it more applicable to all believers, whether male or female (Galatians 3:28). The Greek word for "mutual affection" or "brotherly kindness" is *philadelphia*, which is where the name of the American city was derived, "The City of Brotherly Love."

Adding *philadelphia* love to your faith simply means walking in love toward your brothers and sisters in the Lord with the emphasis on growing in affection, meaning warm feelings.

By contrast, the Greek word for the seventh virtue— "love"—is *agape (ag-AH-pay)*, which doesn't primarily refer to affection, but rather *practical* love.

To understand the difference of these two types of love let's look at **the four types of love**, starting with…

1. *Storge* Love

***Storge* love** is familial love. It's the bond, affection and loyalty that develop between family members. Although the word itself, *storge (STOR-gay),* is not found in the Bible we see numerous examples of it, like Martha & Mary's love for their brother Lazarus in John 11.

Unfortunately family members don't always develop *storge* love for each other and instead develop hatred. A couple examples from the Scriptures are Cain & Abel (Genesis 4:1-11) and Joseph & his jealous brothers (Genesis 37).

2. *Phileo* Love

***Phileo* love** is friendship love or brotherly love like the platonic affection of David and Jonathan (2 Samuel 1:25-26). Both *phileo* (verb) and *philadelphia* (noun) stem from the same word, *philos (FEE-loss),* which refers to a friend or someone who's dearly loved in a non-romantic sense. You could say that *phileo* love is *storge* love applied to non-family members or that *storge* love is *phileo* love applied to family members. In either case, there's an element of "tender affection" or a bond. The word *phileo (fil-LAY-oh)* can be found some 25 times in the original Greek text of the New Testament. The noun form, *philia,* appears much less often.

Jesus' had *phileo* love—that is, warm affection—for Martha, Mary and Lazarus, as observed here:

(5) Now Jesus <u>loved</u> Martha and her sister and Lazarus.

(35) Jesus wept. (36) Then the Jews said, "See how he <u>loved</u> him!"

John 11:5, 35-36

3. *Eros* Love

Eros **love** is *phileo* love between members of the opposite sex, but heightened to a romantic level. It doesn't, however, refer to shallow sexual lust. Although the word *eros (eer-ROSS)* doesn't appear in the original manuscripts there are many examples of this type of love in the Scriptures. One overt instance can be observed in the amazing Song of Songs. Here's a passionate expression of love in that book where the man is speaking to the woman:

> **show me your face,**
> **let me hear your voice;**
> **for your voice is sweet,**
> **and your face is lovely.**
>
> **Song of Songs 2:14**

4. *Agape* Love

Agape **love** is simply practical love or love-in-action and is therefore not dependent on affection (although it obviously includes affection in cases where *phileo* love, *storge* love and *eros* love apply). This can be observed in the Scriptural definition of *agape* love found in 1 Corinthians 13:4-8, which says that *agape* love is patient, kind, does not envy, does not boast, is not proud, is not rude or selfish or easily angered, etc.

The word 'love' in the most popular passage of the Bible is *agape:*

> **"For God so <u>loved</u> the world that he gave**
> **his one and only Son, that whoever believes in**
> **him shall not perish but have eternal life."**
>
> **John 3:16**

The Creator was walking in love toward all humanity when the Father allowed the Son to die in our place as our substitutionary death. This was *agape* love, **practical love**, and not *phileo* love.

Phileo Love is Not Necessary to *Agape* Love

With this understanding, you don't have to have *phileo* love for people—warm affection or respect—to *agape* love them. Why? Because *agape* love refers to practical love and has little to do with affection; that is, liking the person. This explains how we can fulfill Jesus & Paul's instructions to love our enemies (Luke 6:27 & Romans 12:20-21). Do you *like* your enemies, that is, *phileo* love them? Of course you don't. But this isn't a problem because **we are not commanded to *phileo* love our enemies, we're told to *agape* love them**. Are you following? This explains why *agape* love is often defined as "unconditional love" since it is practical in nature and, again, not dependent upon liking an individual or how well they treat you.

However, I should stress that *agape* love does not refer to only the nicey-wicey kind of love. *Agape* love is love-in-action and refers to doing the *kind* thing or *good* thing for the person in question. Are you truly being kind or good by condoning something that will eventually ruin or destroy a person? Or, worse, *enabling* them? This explains how Jesus—who *is* love because "God is love" (1 John 4:8)—was able to chase the fools out of the temple with a whip, yelling and throwing over tables (Mark 11:15-18); or when he rebuked Peter as "Satan" (Matthew 16:23). His actions may not have been nice, but they were kind and good because they benefited the people.[18]

---

[18] See the teaching "Gentle Love and Tough Love" at the Fountain of Life website for more details.

In light of all this, allow me to point something out that you won't hear very often: God *is* agape love and so He loves *(agape)* the world, just as the most popular passages states, John 3:16. What this means is that God is extending practical love to all human beings even though unbelievers are unregenerated "objects of wrath" (Ephesians 2:1-5). I was only saved and "made alive with Christ" because of God's great *agape* love!

However, God doesn't *phileo* love everyone, that is, have tender affection for them. He doesn't have a close bond with everyone. For instance, do you think God is up there observing the many pedophile priests and saying, "Oh, I just have so much warm affection for these sick perverts?" Do you think the LORD was close buddies with Hitler? Of course not. There's so much false teaching about love in the body of Christ because people don't understand the different *types* of love. One doozy is that *agape* love never existed in the human race until spiritual rebirth was made available through Christ. Poppycock! While it's true that spiritual regeneration and the empowerment of the Holy Spirit heightens the believer's ability to walk in *agape* love this doesn't mean practical love didn't exist before the Church Age. People who teach such things apparently never actually read the definition of *agape* love in 1 Corinthians 13:4-8, which we'll look at momentarily.

Come Near to God and He Will Come Near to YOU

The Bible says that the Father *phileo* loved Jesus when Jesus was on earth (John 5:19-20). Why? Because Jesus imitated the Father, that is, he was godly—*like* God. As such, Jesus grew in God's favor (Luke 2:52). We too can grow in God's favor by coming near to Him (James 4:8, 2 Peter 3:18 & Ephesians 5:1).

Think about it in terms of a "teacher's pet," in a positive way. The pupil is the teacher's pet because she honors the teacher and is compliant. She does her homework and strives to do well on tests. If she offends the teacher she readily apologizes. The teacher will naturally have *phileo* love for such a student—affection and respect—but not for a student who's aloof and shows contempt. Of course the teacher will care about the latter student because the noble instructor unbiasedly cares about all his students. He wants each one to learn, mature and be successful in life. But when the student is foolish and disrespectful there's only so much the teacher can do. The teacher will walk in *agape* love toward such students—practical love—but he will not have *phileo* love for them. Why? Because they're fools who regard the teacher with contempt. All the instructor can do is continue walking in *agape* love toward them—including praying for them and tough love when appropriate—in the hope that they'll positively respond at some point and turn from their folly.

Let's relate this to you and God: YOU can grow in God's *phileo* love just like the teacher's pet! "Come near to God and he will draw near to YOU." It's an *axiom*—a universal law. Strive for a closer relationship with your Creator. Cultivate a more intimate prayer life, which is simply talking with the LORD. Paul instructed us to "pray without ceasing," which indicates a 24/7 bond of communion (1 Thessalonians 5:17). Love God by obeying His instructions, both the general instructions from the *written* Word and the specific instructions of the *living* Word, the Spirit of Christ (1 John 5:3). As you do this you'll **grow in God's favor** just as surely as Jesus Christ did when he was on earth (Luke 2:52) and others as well, like Samuel (1 Samuel 2:26). Peter put it like this:

> **But grow in the grace** [i.e. favor] **and**
> **knowledge of our Lord and Savior Jesus Christ.**
> **To him be glory both now and forever! Amen.**
> **2 Peter 3:18**

Just as important as it is to grow in the *knowledge* of the Lord, it's also vital to grow in God's *grace;* that is, his **favor.** DO IT. This is adding godliness to your faith as covered earlier.

Now that you understand the four types of love, let's separately look at adding "mutual affection" and "love" to our faith.

Adding Mutual (Christian) Affection

In the context of 2 Peter 1:7 "mutual affection" refers to loving our brethren and sistren in the Lord. Again, the Greek word for "mutual affection" is *philadelphia*, which corresponds to *phileo* love. The Bible repeatedly encourages us to *phileo* love— *philadelphia* love—our Christian brothers and sisters:

> **Be devoted to one another in <u>love</u> *(philadelphia)*. Honor one another above yourselves.**
>
> **Romans 12:10**

> **Do nothing out of selfish ambition or vain conceit. Rather, <u>in humility value others above yourselves</u>, (4) <u>not looking to your own interests but each of you to the interests of the others</u>.**
>
> **Philippians 2:3-4**

What if every believer started seriously loving his or her fellow Christians by honoring them above himself or herself— selflessly looking to the interests of other believers? It would be revolutionary!

> **Now about your <u>love</u>** *(philadelphia)* **for**
> **one another we do not need to write to you, for**
> **you yourselves have been taught by God to <u>love</u>**
> *(agapaó)* **each other.**
>
>

1 Thessalonians 4:9

Believers are to *phileo* love one another—cultivate tender affection in our relationships. Again, if every believer did this it would be revolutionary!

The second time "love" appears in this verse it's the Greek word *agapaó (ah-gahp-AH-o)*, which is the verb form of *agape*. It's much easier to *agape* love someone when you have *phileo* love for them, which is the way it's supposed to be with all genuine believers. If you find it extremely difficult to muster *phileo* love for someone who *says* they're a Christian, but who is typically obnoxious due to arrogance and fleshly traits it's likely that you're dealing with a wolf in sheep's clothing. Sad but true.

> **Now that you have purified yourselves by**
> **obeying the truth so that you have sincere <u>love</u>**
> *(philadelphia)* **for each other, <u>love</u>** *(agapaó)* **one**
> **another deeply, from the heart.**
>
>

1 Peter 1:22

Let's apply this verse to us: Now that we're spiritually regenerated Christians and therefore have genuine affection— *phileo* love—for our fellow believers let's be sure to *agape* love one another—that is, walk in practical love toward each other— and let it stem from the heart, that is, the warm affection of *phileo* love.

Hebrews 10:24 instructs us to "spur one another on toward love and good deeds." Do this in accordance with your particular grace gifts:

We have different gifts, according to the grace given to each of us. If your gift is <u>prophesying</u>, then prophesy in accordance with your faith; (7) if it is <u>serving</u>, then serve; if it is <u>teaching</u>, then teach; (8) if it is to <u>encourage</u>, then give encouragement; if it is <u>giving</u>, then give generously; if it is to <u>lead</u>, do it diligently; if it is to <u>show mercy</u>, do it cheerfully.

Romans 12:6-8

Utilize whatever gift you have to bless your brothers and sisters in the Lord. My gifts are teaching and encouraging. What are yours?

Adding *Agape* Love

Adding "love" in the context of 2 Peter 1:7 refers to walking in love toward those who are lost and dying in the world. As already noted, the Greek word for 'love' here is *agape*, which refers to practical love as shown in this popular passage:

Love is patient, love is kind. It does not envy, it does not boast, it is not proud. (5) It does not dishonor others, it is not self-seeking, it is not easily angered, it keeps no record of wrongs. (6) Love does not delight in evil but rejoices with the truth. (7) It always protects, always trusts, always hopes, always perseveres.
(8) Love never fails.

1 Corinthians 13:4-8

Allow me to restress an important point: Since *agape* love is practical love, it doesn't require *phileo* love in order to walk in it (or *storge* love or *eros* love). You don't have to have any affection or respect whatsoever toward an individual to *agape* love him or her, which explains Jesus and Paul's instructions to love our enemies. You don't have to have warm feelings or respect for your enemies to *agape* love them because the **Biblical definition of agape love** shows that it's practical in nature.

Nor does *agape* loving someone one mean always being sugary-sweet nice. Yes, *agape* love is kind, but sometimes the kindest thing you can do for a person is boldly tell them the truth. Why? Because only the truth will set him/her free. Christians aren't mandated to be nice; we're mandated to be good. And sometimes doing the good thing for a person or situation isn't the nice thing; but it is the right thing, as long as you're led of the Holy Spirit.

That said, you should only take the tough love route if it's absolutely necessary and more gentle measures have proven ineffective.

The Bible encourages us to add *agape* love to our faith because it's easy to get saved, hook up with a fellowship/sect and not have much to do with unsaved people. It's so easy to get preoccupied with activities within Christian circles that we forget about the multitudes captive and hurting in this lost, dying world. There are Christians who pretty much refuse to have anything to do with unbelievers, not unlike the Israelites during Jesus' era who shunned Samaritans. Let's not be like that! Jesus wasn't. He went out of his way to talk with the outcast Samaritan woman and ministered to her (John 4:4-26). He *agape* loved her. Even though Christ was called specifically to "the lost sheep of Israel" he ministered to a Canaanite woman and, indirectly, her daughter (Matthew 15:21-28).

What are some ways that you can *agape* love unbelievers? Pray for them regularly, consider ways to bless them, do a good deed, share the message of Christ, "turn the cheek" when necessary and, by all means, don't be a Pharisaical hypocrite.

Here's a good passage:

> **But in your hearts revere Christ as Lord. Always be prepared to give an answer to everyone who asks you to give the reason for the hope that you have. But do this with gentleness and respect,**
>
> **1 Peter 3:15**

The important thing is that you don't forget the lost on your Christian pilgrimage and act like they don't exist. Be sure to *agape* love them!

Adding the Seven Virtues Guarantees Spiritual Growth

This ends our study of the seven virtues from 2 Peter 1:2-11. The passage encourages us to "make every effort" to add these qualities to our faith because they guarantee spiritual effectiveness, productivity and growth. It's no accident that there are seven virtues because the number 7 signifies completeness or completion. Notice what Paul said to the Philippian believers on this:

> **I thank my God every time I remember you. (4) In all my prayers for all of you, I always pray with joy (5) because of your partnership in the gospel from the first day until now, (6) being confident of this, that <u>he who began a good work in you will carry it on to completion</u> until the day of Christ Jesus.**
>
> **Philippians 1:3-6**

While Paul was confident that the Lord would carry on to completion the good work He started in the believers at Philippi, it would only happen *if* they were attentive to adding the seven virtues to their faith. Do you want to be productive in your Christian walk and go on to maturity, to completion? Of course you do. Then diligently add these qualities to your faith on a regular basis!

Chapter Nine

Establishing a Solid Foundation

Establishing a sound spiritual foundation in STAGE TWO is important because it sets the groundwork for the believer's entire walk with the Lord. Just as a good foundation is a prerequisite for a sound building, so a proper spiritual foundation is vital for an effective, liberating and victorious Christian life. People who fail to lay a proper foundation are doomed to spiritual immaturity because they have nothing by which to judge what is right or wrong, scriptural or unscriptural, appropriate or inappropriate, wise or foolish. A heathy biblical understructure eliminates feeble spirituality.

Believers who fail to establish a good foundation during STAGE TWO can shipwreck their faith altogether, as Paul put it in 1 Timothy 1:19, and find themselves back in STAGE ONE—in spiritual darkness and separate from God. That's why these next two chapters exist. They'll help believers lay a quality understructure so that their faith isn't shipwrecked at some point down the road.

The Six Basic Doctrines

Many Christians don't know this, but the Bible details six doctrines that will ensure a sound spiritual foundation:

> **Therefore let us move beyond the elementary teachings about Christ and be taken forward to maturity, not laying again THE FOUNDATION of <u>repentance from acts that lead to death</u>, and of <u>faith in God</u>, (2) <u>instruction about baptisms</u>, the <u>laying on of hands</u>, the <u>resurrection of the dead</u>, and <u>eternal judgment</u>.**
> **Hebrews 6:1-2**

The writer of Hebrews was lamenting that the believers he was addressing needed to be taught these basic doctrines all over again when they should've been teachers by this point (Hebrews 5:11-12). Notice that knowing these six elementary doctrines is spoken of in terms of "laying" a "foundation." In other words, these teachings are the **elementary understructure** for every Christian. They are as follows:

1. Repentance from acts that lead to death.
2. Faith in God.
3. Instructions about baptisms.
4. The laying on of hands.
5. The resurrection of the dead.
6. Eternal judgment.

When you fully understand these basic doctrines no one will be able to lead you astray with false doctrine. For instance, some Christians falsely teach that it's not necessary for believers to keep in repentance, but the very first elementary doctrine contradicts this. Some say that spiritual rebirth isn't biblical, but the third doctrine disproves this. Some say that everyone will ultimately be saved regardless of the evil they chose to practice without repentance, but the sixth doctrine refutes this. Simply put, the six basic doctrines will protect you from doctrinal error.

Years ago I did a six-part series on these foundational doctrines, one sermon per each teaching. A knowledgeable minister could easily do a *series* of teachings on every one of them. Unbelievably, in most Christian camps the six basic doctrines are almost utterly ignored. And then ministers wonder why many in their congregations act like spiritual babies. It's because the pastors and teachers aren't properly feeding them! This means, of course, that they're not doing their jobs (Ephesians 4:11-14 & 1 Peter 5:1-4).

Since an entire book could be written on the six basic doctrines, I'm not going to go into exhaustive detail on them. However, it is necessary to go into *some* detail to be effective. The purpose of these chapters is to simply provide foundational structure for younger believers, as well as help more mature believers inspect and fix their foundation as necessary. Speaking of which…

In Chapter Three I emphasized that no believer is in bondage to their foundation that was laid during STAGE TWO. If you come across more accurate biblical data you should adjust your foundation accordingly. I've come across believers who won't change their view on this or that subject because it goes against "how they were taught," no matter how much scriptural evidence is offered to the contrary. This is immaturity where the believer puts the word of some pastor or sect above the Word of God. Please don't be like this. At the same time you shouldn't make changes to your foundation at a whim. Don't make any adjustments or repairs until doing a thorough biblical investigation, like the Bereans did when Paul preached the message of Christ to them (Acts 17:10-12). The truth will set you free (John 8:31-32).

Let's now look at each of the six basic doctrines:

1. Repentance from Acts that Lead to Death

The word 'repent' simply means to change one's mind for the positive. What are we to repent of? "Acts that lead to death." The word 'act' is the same Greek word translated as "act" in this passage:

> The **acts** <u>**of the flesh**</u> **are obvious: sexual immorality, impurity and debauchery; (20) idolatry and witchcraft; hatred, discord, jealousy, fits of rage, selfish ambition, dissensions, factions (21) and envy; drunkenness, orgies, and the like. I warn you, as I did before, that those who live like this will not inherit the kingdom of God.**
>
> **Galatians 5:19-21**

These verses show that "acts of the flesh" aren't limited to just sexual immorality, drunkard-ness, stealing and murder. Things like discord (strife), jealousy, factions, hatred and envy are also works of the flesh. Unfortunately, they're regularly evident in many congregations. Paul warns believers that "those **who live like this** will not inherit the kingdom of God," meaning those who practice these sins with no care to repent. This explains why the Bible encourages us to keep 'fessed-up when we miss it:

> **If we claim to be without sin, we deceive ourselves and the truth is not in us. (9)** <u>**If**</u> **we confess our sins, he is faithful and just and will forgive us our sins and purify us from all unrighteousness.**
>
> **1 John 1:8-9**

When we miss it we need to be quick to repent. This takes humility, of course, but humility is good because **God's favor flows to the humble, not the proud**. In fact, the LORD *resists* or *opposes* the proud, which is why He doesn't offer forgiveness to the unrepentant (James 4:6 & 1 Peter 5:5). This explains Jesus' declaration: "But **unless you repent** you will all perish" (Luke 13:3,5). Arrogant people have an extremely hard time admitting they're wrong, which is why they won't repent. By contrast, humble folk will readily confess when missing it and it's humility that unlocks God's favor.

John the Baptist referred to regularly repenting as "keeping with repentance":

> **"Produce   fruit   in   <u>keeping   with</u> <u>repentance</u>."**
> **Matthew & Luke 3:8**

It's impossible to bear fruit unto God while knowingly walking in unrepentant sin. So **the principle of keeping with repentance assures the continuing stream of the LORD's forgiveness and favor in our lives as we repent**. Needless to say, don't allow unconfessed sin to block-up your spiritual arteries from the flow of God's grace.

Humbly 'fessing-up should become a regular activity in the life of the believer. It's particularly helpful for believers who are in bondage to a certain sin. They want free, but they keep falling back into the sin in question and confessing. This keeping-with-repentance principle ensures the flow of the LORD's forgiveness and favor into their lives. As they seek God and continue in His Word they will eventually walk in freedom (see <u>Chapter Eleven</u> for details). I was once one of these people, but no longer struggle with any certain sin, which is different than saying I never miss it. A couple days ago I missed it and felt so convicted; I immediately repented and received God's grace. Praise God!

The question is often raised: How long can a believer knowingly continue in sin without repentance before God cuts him or her off from salvation? Surely God overflows with mercy, patience and compassion and, as such, there's a generous "grace period." How long is this grace period? Jesus' Parable of the Barren Fig Tree addresses the question. In this story, from Luke 13:5-9, the owner of the vineyard represents God, the fruitless fig tree represents an individual in covenant with God who's not bearing fruit, the caretaker of the vineyard represents Jesus, the mediator between the owner and the fig tree. In the story the owner wants to cut the tree down because it hasn't produced fruit in *three years*, but the caretaker intercedes and convinces the owner to give the tree *one more year* wherein the caretaker will do everything he can to get it to be fruitful. If the tree still hasn't produced fruit by the end of the fourth year the owner and caretaker agree to cut it down and remove it from the vineyard. What we see here is patience, mercy and grace. The owner of the vineyard and the caretaker, who represent the heavenly Father and Jesus, are willing to give the tree a total of *four years* to be fruitful before ultimately cutting it down, and that would only be because they must.

The story is figurative so we can't take it strictly literal, i.e. that God will pluck someone out of the kingdom if they're fruitless for exactly four years. What we *can* get from it, however, is that God's patience, mercy and grace are awesome and He will do everything He can to get us to be fruitful. He's invested in us greatly and understandably wants us to be productive. Another thing we can get from the parable is that when the Lord's mercy ends His judgment begins and he'll cut off when/if necessary. Why be foolish and incur such judgment?

So, while there's no doubt to God's great mercy and grace in such cases, why risk walking on thin ice by playing around with sin? Particularly in view of such sobering passages as Galatians 5:19-21, Hebrews 10:26-27 and 2 Peter 2:20-21. Some are deceived into thinking they can flirt with the flesh—the deceptive beast within us all—but before they know it they become captive to it. This is the deceitfulness of sin noted in Hebrews 3:12-14. Sin has the power to harden a person's heart to the point where s/he doesn't want anything to do with God or the things of God. How so? Practice a carnal behavior long enough without care of repentance and there comes a point where character is firmly set and nigh incorrigible. Pathological liars are testimony to this.

Someone might argue that Jesus died on the cross for our past, present *and* future sins and therefore it's not technically necessary to keep in repentance to be forgiven of future sins. While it's true that Jesus died for our future sins along with our past and present ones, you can't very well repent of something you haven't even done yet, which is why 1 John 1:8-9 is in the Bible.[19]

Why is the first basic doctrine referred to in terms of repenting from fleshly works "that lead to death"? Because death is the wages of sin (Romans 6:23). Sin leads to death!

While it's clear that the first basic doctrine refers to repenting of works of the flesh, the terminology in the Greek is open enough to interpret it as "repentance from dead works," which is how the KJV and ESV put it. As such, the first basic doctrine includes repenting from dead religious works performed to obtain reconciliation with God and eternal salvation. This, by the way, is the definition of human-made religion, which Jesus said doesn't work. We covered this in Chapter One but let's briefly address it again: When the disciples asked Jesus who could be saved, he responded:

> **"With people it is impossible, but not with God; for all things are possible with God."**
> **Mark 10:27**

---

[19] For important details on this topic see the teaching "Once Saved Always Saved?" at the Fountain of Life website. Also see chapter 3 of *The Believer's Guide to Forgiveness & Warfare*.

Eternal salvation and everything that goes with it—
reconciliation with the LORD, forgiveness of sins and the
acquisition of eternal life—are only available through God and not
human religion, including religious "Christianity," which isn't
actual Christianity. These awesome blessings are available
exclusively from God through the gospel, which explains why
'gospel' literally means "good news."

The first doctrine of Christianity is to repent of—and keep
in repentance of—acts of the sinful nature and dead religious
works. This is why the gospel is referred to as **repentance unto
life**" in the Bible (Acts 11:18). Enough said.

2. Faith in God

Faith in God is the second basic doctrine because, as the
Bible says:

> **And without faith it is impossible to
> please God, because anyone who comes to him
> must believe that he exists and that he rewards
> those who earnestly seek him.**
> **Hebrews 11:6**

Faith is vital because without it it's impossible to please
God. What exactly is faith?

Faith is belief, but not in the sense of believing in fairy
tales or casual mental assent. It's belief based on **1.** what is
intrinsically obvious, **2.** accurate knowledge, whether scientific,
spiritual or otherwise, **3.** genuine revelation by the Holy Spirit, or
4. some combination of these three.

Let's consider examples of the first three. Regarding #1,
someone may say they believe in the concept of God as Creator
because it's obvious that the earth, universe and all living creatures
were intelligently designed. Or someone may believe

homosexuality is intrinsically wrong because the design and function of the sexual organs is obvious (tab 'A' fits into slot 'B'). In each case the person believes based on what is clearly palpable. Concerning #2, people may believe they have a brain even though they've never seen it because medical science has proven it through dissecting human remains, brain surgery, etc. So the person believes based on sound data. Regarding #3, some may turn to God because the Holy Spirit revealed reality to them and they believed it. Their belief is based on the enlightenment of the Holy Spirit.

The Bible calls faith the substance of things hoped for and being certain of what we do not see (Hebrews 11:1). The Amplified Bible amplifies the original Greek text:

> Now **faith is the assurance (the confirmation, the title deed) of the things [we] hope for**, being the proof of things [we] do not see *and* the conviction of their reality [faith perceiving as real fact what is not revealed to the senses].
>
> **Hebrews 11:1** (Amplified)

Faith is the "**title deed**" of the things we hope for; that is, the things we righteously desire. In short, **faith is the substance that brings the world of hope or desire into reality**! In the Gospels, for instance, people would come to Jesus hoping for healing and after receiving it the Lord would say something like "Your faith has healed you" (see, for example, Mark 5:25-34). Faith was the substance that brought them what they hoped for, healing. They were certain—convinced—that Jesus would heal them even though they couldn't yet see it physically.

I trust you're seeing why faith is necessary to receive God's gracious gift of reconciliation and eternal life. After all, how can someone receive a gift from someone he/she doesn't even believes exists? For example, if you said you had a gift for me and I responded by saying I can't receive it because I don't believe you exist, would you still force the gift on me? Of course not. More likely, you'd be irked at my stupidity and arrogance. The same principle applies to those who reject the gospel. When you come across people who do this, be sure to pray that the LORD open their eyes to the truth, i.e. reality.

Did you ever wonder why faith is so important to receiving salvation? Because **faith is nothing more or less than believing God**. That's precisely what Adam & Eve failed to do when they were tested in the Garden of Eden and that's why they fell (see Genesis 2:15-3:24). In other words, **the fall of humanity came about due to unbelief and therefore humanity's restoration is dependent upon belief**.

In a sense, every human soul has faith, which explains why we're incurably religious as a species (even those who claim to not believe in God develop belief systems and institutions that have all the earmarks of what is generally perceived as "religion"[20]). Belief in God is simply a part of our make-up; it's in our spiritual DNA. Heck, creation itself inspires belief in God; more than that, creation *screams out* God's existence (Psalm 19:1-4 & Romans 1:18-20). To suggest that everything in the universe came about through accident and that there's no Intelligent Designer is like expecting a Boeing 747 to emerge out of a metal scrapyard after millions of years. It's absurd. Unfortunately, as Paul put it, unbelievers "are darkened in their understanding and separated from the life of God because of the ignorance that is in them due to the hardening of

---

[20] For instance, secular humanism—essentially one-in-the-same as far left "liberalism"—has its own cosmology, its own miracles, its own beliefs in the supernatural, its own "churches" (public schools), its own "high priests" (godless professors and teachers), its own "saints" (thugs), its own worldview and its own explanation of the existence of the universe. While this is generally true, it *shouldn't* be interpreted to mean that I'm against all professors, public school teachers, scientists, etc. because this *isn't* true in the least.

their hearts" (Ephesians 4:18). In other words, they have faith but they've willingly hardened their hearts to it, consciously or subconsciously. Why? For a number of reasons, such as not wanting to give up some pet sin, but often simply because that's how their godless culture brainwashed them and they choose to run with the pack. And so they deny obvious reality.

Repentance and Faith

It's interesting that repentance and faith are the first two basic doctrines of Christianity because **these are the conditions to receiving God's gift of eternal salvation**:

> **I have declared to both Jews and Greeks that they must turn to God in <u>repentance</u> and have <u>faith</u> in our Lord Jesus.**
>
> **Acts 20:21**

We effectively "turn to God" via the gospel **through repentance and faith**.

'Repentance' inexplicably has a negative connotation in modern times because people misinterpret it to mean that God is trying to prevent them from having a "good time." But sin can only bring a "good time" superficially because underneath the surface pleasure is misery and death for "the wages of sin is death." This is an **axiom.**

Take, for instance, the "party" lifestyle. When I was a teen I smoked pot, did drugs and drank frequently. It became a lifestyle and it was difficult for me to imagine life without constant "partying." After several years I wisely quit. This was before I even became a believer. In essence, I repented because repentance is simply the resolve to change for the positive and the corresponding action. Why did I quit? Because, although doing these things delivered a quick fix to escape reality and have a "good time," they couldn't deliver the goods in the long term. Instead they brought hangovers, depression, broken relationships and bondage.

What spurred my change-for-the-positive, i.e. repentance? I saw the obvious truth, believed it, and changed accordingly. The same principle applies to receiving God's grace of salvation through the gospel of Christ. We see the truth, believe it, and change accordingly. **Repentance is the resolve to change for the positive in accordance with God's will**.

Our covenant is a covenant of faith and so everything in our covenant is by faith. Do you want eternal salvation? It's by faith. Healing? It's by faith. Intimacy with God? Faith. Answers to prayer? Faith. Power to overcome? Faith.

In light of this I find it perplexing when I come across Christians who are "anti-faith" because it's a total oxymoron. They defend their position on the grounds that there have been some extremists in the faith movement, but every movement in the body of Christ inspired by the Holy Spirit has its lunatic fringe. You don't throw the baby out with the bathwater!

One thing about faith needs to be stressed, which was covered in Chapter Seven: **Faith must be combined with perseverance—i.e. patient endurance—or what you're hoping for will not come to pass**. This is why the Bible says:

> **We do not want you to become lazy, but to imitate those who <u>through faith and patience</u> inherit what has been promised.**
> **Hebrews 6:12**

After all, faith isn't really faith if you give up. It might be temporary, fleeting faith, but it's not the faith that can withstand the time of testing, which includes the wait before the manifestation (Luke 8:13). I provided some examples from my own life in Chapter Seven so let me just emphasize that even salvation can be lost if one doesn't persevere in the faith, as shown in this passage

> **Once you were alienated from God and were enemies in your minds because of your evil behavior. (22) But now he has reconciled you by Christ's physical body through death to present you holy in his sight, without blemish and free from accusation—(23) if you continue in your faith, established and firm, and do not move from the hope held out in the gospel.**
>
> **Colossians 1:21-23**

One last thing about the second basic doctrine: Someone might argue that it's technically "faith **in God**" and therefore only refers to believing the LORD personally. Yes, it refers to believing God personally, but it also includes whatever God has created that testifies to His existence or will. For instance, all creation is a physical testimony to the existence of the Almighty and therefore inspires faith. One of the reasons I was an agnostic and not a strict atheist before I accepted the message of Christ is because the earth & universe and all living things screamed out that there was an Intelligent Designer. I simply wasn't stupid enough to be an atheist. Consider also the testimony of God's amazing Word: The Lord is truth and His Word is truth and therefore His Word testifies to His existence (John 14:6 & 17:17).

3. Instructions about Baptisms

The third basic doctrine is biblical teachings about baptisms. The Greek word for 'baptize' is *baptizó (bap-TID-zoh)*, meaning "to submerse or dip." The noun form is in the plural in Hebrews 6:2 because there are three baptisms in Christianity. Most Christians only know about water baptism, which ironically is the least important (which is different than saying it's unimportant). Every believer should experience all three baptisms, but the first one *must* be experienced to be a Christian. The three baptisms are:

1. Baptism into Christ
2. Water baptism.
3. The baptism of the Holy Spirit.

Let's address all three:

Baptism into Christ

This refers to being *spiritually* born-again through Christ. Notice what the Scriptures say about this baptism:

> **So in Christ Jesus you are all children of God through faith, (27) for all of you who were <u>baptized into Christ</u> have clothed yourselves with Christ.**
>
> **Galatians 3:26-27**

> **He saved us, not because of righteous things we had done, but because of his mercy. He saved us through <u>the washing of rebirth</u> and renewal by the Holy Spirit**
>
> **Titus 3:5**

The reason the baptism into Christ is a foundational doctrine is because it's impossible to be a Christian apart from this new spiritual birth. If someone says they're a believer, but aren't spiritually regenerated then they're a Christian in name only and aren't genuinely saved.

If you come across any minister or group that says people don't have to be spiritually reborn to be Christians, as Jesus stressed in John 3:3,6, they should be rejected as false teachers. As Jesus said about the false teachers of his day: "Leave them; they are blind guides. If the blind lead the blind, both will fall into a pit" (Matthew 15:14).

Water Baptism

Baptism in water is simply a *public testimony* of the believer's baptism into Christ. Acts 10:47-48 is a good example. Four things about water baptism you should know:

1. It is an outward expression of a personal decision already made.
2. It doesn't symbolize washing, but rather death, death to the sin nature.
3. Being lifted out of the water symbolizes resurrection to a new life.
4. Believers are to be baptized "in the name of the Father and of the Son and of the Holy Spirit" (Matthew 28:19).

I'm sure you see why water baptism isn't as important as the baptism into Christ since water baptism is merely the symbolic testimony of *what has already taken place spiritually through the baptism into Christ*. What's more important, the inward baptism or the outward baptism that represents it?

Baptism of the Holy Spirit

Being baptized into Christ is essentially one-in-the-same as being "born of the Spirit" (John 3:3,6), but being born of the Spirit is distinct from the baptism of the Spirit, although they can occasionally happen at the same time. When you're born of the Spirit, the Spirit is *in* you (Romans 8:9 & 1 Corinthians 6:19), whereas when you're baptized in the Spirit, the Spirit is *all over you* because you're immersed with the Spirit. It's the difference between drinking a glass of water and jumping into a lake. Think about it.

Speaking in tongues is the *initial physical evidence* of the baptism of the Holy Spirit. While speaking in tongues is not the Holy Spirit and the Holy Spirit is not speaking in tongues, *they go hand in hand.* Here are five scriptural examples of people receiving this baptism:

1. **The believers in Jerusalem, as shown in Acts 2:1-4.** All of them spoke in tongues.
2. **The Samaritans, as shown in Acts 8:12-19.** The Samaritans were part Jew and part Gentile. Verse 18 shows that Simon the sorcerer "saw" that the Spirit was given to the Samaritans when the apostles laid their hands on them. In other words, he saw evidence that they received the Holy Spirit. What did he see? We must interpret Scripture with Scripture, which is a hermeneutical rule. Since the rest of the New Testament shows that speaking in tongues is the initial evidence of the baptism of the Holy Spirit, this must've been what Simon saw—people speaking in languages they didn't know.
3. **Saul in Damascus, as shown in Acts 9:17-18.** Although speaking in tongues is not mentioned in this passage, the baptism of the Holy Spirit is, and we observe scriptural evidence elsewhere that Saul (Paul) spoke in tongues on a regular basis, which is praying in the spirit (1 Corinthians 14:18-19).
4. **Cornelius' household in Caesarea, as shown in Acts 10:44-48.** This refers to the first Gentile believers. Verses 45-46 state that "The circumcised believers who had come with Peter were astonished that the gift of the Holy Spirit had been poured out even on the Gentiles. *For they heard*

them speaking in tongues and praising God." Since believers who are not baptized in the spirit can and do praise God, the evidence of the baptism is obviously speaking in tongues.

5. **The Ephesians, as shown in Acts 19:5-7.** This passage shows that all twelve spoke in tongues as a result of receiving the baptism, not just a select few.

As already noted *every* Christian can and should receive this baptism and pray in the spirit to supplement prayer in his or her everyday language. This can be observed in 1 Corinthians 14:14-15, 18-19 and Ephesians 6:18. I have to emphasize this because there's this idea rampant in the body of Christ that speaking in tongues was done away with once the biblical canon was completed. Don't believe it; it's a colossal lie that has allowed the enemy to keep multitudes of sincere believers from the *full* empowerment and help of the Holy Spirit.

Praying in the spirit is important because it edifies us by building us up in faith and empowers us to witness, to love people and to walk free from sin, which we'll look at momentarily.

Before we do, there are a few things about the baptism of the Spirit and speaking in tongues that should be stressed and clarified:

- Just because a Christian is baptized in the Spirit and *can* speak in tongues it does not mean that he or she is walking in the spirit; that is, bearing fruit of the spirit, like love, joy, peace, kindness, faith, humility and self-control (Galatians 5:22-23). Putting it another way, to be spirit-controlled is synonymous with bearing fruit of the spirit but just because a believer is baptized in the Spirit and can speak in tongues doesn't mean that he or she is participating in the divine nature, i.e. walking in the spirit and producing the fruit thereof (2 Peter 1:4).

- If a Christian can walk in the spirit to a good degree *without* the baptism of the Holy Spirit, how much more so if they *are* baptized in the Holy Spirit! In other words, just because you're doing well spiritually without speaking in tongues, don't let it rob you of this wonderful gift that God has provided for all believers!

- The baptism of the Holy Spirit is usually transferred through physical contact via the ministry of the laying on of hands, but not always. Although the gift can be received in this manner through someone who already has it, as shown in some of the above examples, a believer can also receive it simply through faith (Luke 11:9-13). In fact, everything in our covenant is by faith.

- If any believer has hands laid on them for this baptism and they don't speak in tongues it doesn't necessarily mean they didn't receive the baptism. They may have received it, but they simply have yet to speak in tongues. We have to understand that speaking in tongues—praying in the spirit—is something that the believer does by his or her volition and is not something the Holy Spirit makes people do. Remember what Paul said: "So what shall *I* do? *I will* pray with my spirit, but *I will* also pray with my mind" (1 Corinthians 14:15). Just as praying in a language you understand is an act of your own will, so is praying in the spirit. With this understanding, if I chose to I could theoretically *not* pray in the spirit the rest of my life even though I'm baptized in the Spirit.

- On that note, there are too many Christians who are baptized in the Spirit and yet rarely if ever pray in the spirit and therefore lack the empowerment the Holy Spirit wants to give them. Speaking of which…

The Empowerment and Help of the Holy Spirit

The reason I'm going into so much detail about the baptism of the Holy Spirit and praying in the spirit is because they are God-given sources of great empowerment for the believer to walk in newness of life and victory. Unfortunately, many believers settle for less than God's best and they go through life struggling with things they don't need to struggle with because the LORD has provided them the power and help they need—if only they knew of these truths and implemented them! This is the very reason God detailed these truths in His Word and it's why I'm stressing them here.

With this understanding, notice the power that Paul said was available for his protégé Timothy:

> **For this reason I remind you to fan into flame the gift of God, which is in you through the laying on of hands. (7) For God did not give us a spirit of timidity, but a spirit of <u>power</u>, of <u>love</u> and of <u>self-discipline</u>.**
>
> **2 Timothy 1:6-7**

What gift was Paul talking about? He doesn't say, but there are clues: The gift was given through the laying on of hands and it is linked to the spirit or Spirit.[21] Since Scripture interprets Scripture we must conclude that Paul was referring to the baptism of the Spirit because **1.** this gift involves the Spirit and **2.** there's repeated evidence that this gift is typically transferred through the

---

[21] Keeping in mind that there was no capitalization in the original Greek and so translators have to determine whether the Greek word for 'spirit'—*pneuma (NYOO-ma)*—refers to the human spirit (un-capitalized) or the Holy Spirit (capitalized).

laying on of hands, as detailed in the previous section. As such, the baptism of the Spirit is the obvious answer.

By instructing Timothy to "fan into flame" this gift he was simply encouraging him to pray in the spirit more often, which is actually the seventh piece of the armor of God (Ephesians 6:18). What does he mean by fan it into flame? Speaking from experience, when I first received the baptism of the Holy Spirit in 1986—two and a half years after my salvation—I would keep saying the same phrase over and over in the spirit. It was just a handful of words and I had no idea what I was saying. Regardless, I put into practice this passage: I fanned the gift into flame by praying in the spirit whenever I had the opportunity, like driving to classes or to work or when I went off by myself to pray, as Jesus did (Luke 5:16). In time my spiritual prayer language grew dramatically. How so? Because I fanned it into flame as Paul instructed. This is the key to walking in the blessings cited in verse 7: **power**, **love** and **self-discipline**.

1. **Power.** The Greek word for 'power' is *dunamis (DOO-nah-miss)* and it's where we get the English word dynamite. When you pray in the spirit you're building yourself up in dynamite power! The more you pray in the spirit the more you'll be empowered—anointed—to fulfill whatever mission the LORD gives you. As you grow you'll kiss timidity goodbye!

2. **Love.** As you pray in the spirit you'll build yourself up in *agape (ah-GAH-pay)* love, which is simply *practical* love, as detailed in Chapter Eight. Hence, you'll be able to practically love people whom you don't even like, including enemies. Put another way, you'll be empowered to love people for whom you don't have loving feelings. By doing this you'll fulfill the biblical instruction to love your enemies (Luke 6:35), which—I always stress—includes *tough* love when appropriate.

3. **Self-Discipline.** As you pray in the spirit you'll also be built up in self-discipline, which means self-control. You'll find yourself being able to do things you never had the discipline to do previously. You'll be empowered to quit negative behaviors or addictions that you've struggled with for years. I'm living proof. In short, it'll give you the edge to win spiritually.

I'm sure you see why the baptism of the Holy Spirit is a foundational doctrine. Christians who write off this incredible gift due to the false doctrine that charismatic gifts passed away with the last of the original apostles are robbing themselves. And believers who have the gift but don't "fan it into flame" are wasting it and robbing themselves of great power and anointing that would enable them to walk in newness of life.

4. The Laying on of Hands

The doctrine of the laying on of hands refers to the transference of four things through physical contact: **1.** blessing, **2.** anointing and consecration for service (ministry), **3.** the baptism of the Holy Spirit, and **4.** healing and deliverance.

Let's briefly look at all four.

Blessing (or General Prayer)

Jesus placed his hands on children and blessed them (Mark 10:13,16 & Matthew 19:13,15). To 'bless' someone means "to speak positive words that have a productive impact." The official priestly prayer supports this definition (Numbers 6:22-27) and you can find these types of prayer/blessings all over the Bible, e.g. Romans 15:13 and Colossians 1:9-12.

Blessing or prayer in this manner is so important because words "have the power of life and death" (Proverbs 18:21). Whether people know it or not, our words bring *life* or *death*, *blessing* or *cursing*. Proverbs 12:18 reinforces this: "Reckless words pierce like a sword, but the tongue of the wise brings healing."

Needless to say, the idea that "words can never hurt me" is a lie.

Kids and youth are especially vulnerable to "reckless words" or verbal abuse, particularly from authority figures in their lives (Colossians 3:21). Adults who continually berate, belittle and call children names are speaking a prophecy of death and destruction over them (!).

Blessing, by contrast, is a prophecy of life, which is why Jesus laid his hands on children and blessed them.

Words are powerful by themselves and adding the dimension of touch magnifies their impact.

See *The Power of the Tongue* in <u>Chapter Seven</u> for more details.

Anointing/Separation for Ministry

Hands are to be lain on those called of God to special service. Biblical examples include the Levites (Numbers 8:10-11), Joshua, (Numbers 27:18-23), Stephen & six others (Acts 6:1-6) and Saul & Barnabas (Acts 13:2-3).

Obviously the people who qualify for such a rite of passage should already be full of faith, God's Word and the Spirit, as was the case with Joshua and Steven in the aforementioned examples. The laying on of hands simply provides a stronger anointing to fulfill their God-given assignment.

Paul instructed his young protégé, Timothy, to not be "hasty in the laying on of hands" (1 Timothy 5:22) because ministers must be **tested** for *character* and *faithfulness* and there's no test like the test of **time**. Those who hastily confirm untested ministers share responsibility for the damage they eventually do to people.

The Holy Spirit Baptism

Hands are to be laid on believers to receive the baptism of the Holy Spirit, which is evidenced by speaking in tongues (Acts 19:1-7).

While this powerful gift is typically received this way—i.e. through someone who has it—a believer can also receive it simply through faith in God's Word (Luke 11:9-13). In other words, believers don't absolutely need a human conduit for the gift to be transferred. We'll look at this more in the next section.

For details on the Holy Spirit baptism and glossolalia see the earlier sections *Baptism of the Holy Spirit* and *The Empowerment and Help of the Holy Spirit.*

Healing and Spiritual Deliverance

Jesus said that believers "will place their hands on sick people, and they will get well" (Mark 16:17-18).

The book of Acts says "God anointed Jesus of Nazareth with the Holy Spirit and power, and… he went around doing good and healing all who were under the power of the devil, because God was with him" (Acts 10:38). We see evidence of this throughout the Gospels. Here are some examples plus important additional info:

- Jesus laid hands on sick people and healed them or exorcized demons from them (Luke 4:40-41).
- A woman who was subject to bleeding for twelve years heard about Jesus' anointing to heal and therefore had faith

to receive healing from him (Mark 5:25-34). When the woman touched his cloak Jesus sensed "power had gone out from him" (verse 30).

- Jesus had an anointing to heal, but his ministry was very limited in his hometown because of the people's lack of faith due to a "spirit of familiarity"—meaning they were so familiar with Jesus during his first three decades that they couldn't acknowledge his divine anointing and receive from it (Mark 6:1-6). This example reveals that receiving a healing is a matter of faith in regards to the person praying (i.e. the human conduit of God's power), as well as the recipient of the healing, which shows that receiving a healing via a human conduit involves a *combination* of faith. Needless to say, there's **power** in agreement (Matthew 18:20 & Leviticus 26:8).

- People with the **greatest faith** do not require hands to be laid on them for healing or deliverance. This type of faith accepts the LORD at His Word, like the centurion from Matthew 8:5-10,13. In other words, they don't require a human conduit to receive healing or deliverance from God. As noted earlier, the Baptism of the Holy Spirit can be received this way (Luke 11:13).

Important Points on Transmitting the Anointing

Here are several things to keep in mind when you lay hands on people to bless, pray, heal or deliver:

- Only make physical contact when you are ready to release your faith.
- While praying over someone you will sense your faith reaching its peak; that's when you should make contact.

- Children may freak out a bit when you lay hands on them because the anointing—God's power—is new to them, but don't let it derail you. Be at peace and keep ministering in faith, as led of the Holy Spirit.

- God's anointing is like electricity flowing through you and your hand is the conductor for this power like an electricity cable.

- When you experience the anointing you'll naturally get excited, which is great; just be careful not to absorb it through excessive shouting, laughing and leaping; rather *channel it* to those who need it. In short, don't waste the anointing—get your hands on someone!

- Since your words and hands are the primary vehicles in which the Spirit transmits the anointing to others don't waste words or motions. Watch your words and actions and be careful not to do anything that will drain or lose the anointing, including grieving the Holy Spirit (Ephesians 4:30).

- Put your words and motions in a direct line and use them to bring healing or deliverance to those in need. It's akin to using a rifle: You aim it at the appropriate target in order to hit it. Wasting words and motions will cause you to miss the target.

- If you want God's power to operate strongly in your life, as was the case with the Christ (Acts 10:38), you must discipline yourself to spend time with the LORD. In other words, saturate yourself with God through praise, worship, the Word and prayer. You can't run around gabbing and doing frivolous things—watching TV, playing golf or computer games, etc.—right before a ministry engagement and expect the anointing to be strong when you minister.

- The anointing flows out of your inmost being like rivers of living water out of the very core of your soul/spirit (John

7:37-39). As such, you must **protect the anointing** so that it'll be there when you need it.

- You can't give something if you don't have it and therefore you can't expect the anointing to flow out of you if you haven't prepared yourself beforehand to operate in God's power. You must never allow people or things to rob you of your worship/Word/prayer time, particularly before you're scheduled to minister. Turn off your phone.

Most Christians unfortunately don't know much about the laying on of hands. This section reveals its importance.

Chapter Ten

Establishing a Solid Foundation Part 2

Continuing with the six basic doctrines (Hebrews 6:1-2):

5. The Resurrection of the Dead

The fifth basic doctrine is the resurrection of the dead, which means that everyone will be bodily resurrected, both the righteous and the unrighteous, as Jesus and Paul plainly declared:

> "for a time is coming when all who are in their graves will hear his voice (29) and come out—those who have done what is good will <u>rise to live</u>, and those who have done what is evil will <u>rise to be condemned</u>."

> **John 5:28-29**

> having hope toward God, which they
> themselves also wait for, that there is about to be
> a <u>rising again of the dead</u>, both of <u>righteous</u> and
> <u>unrighteous</u>;
>
> **Acts 24:15** (YLT)

As you can see, there will be resurrections of both the righteous and unrighteous. This doesn't mean, however, that there will only be two resurrections in number, just that there are two *types* of resurrections: **1.** The resurrection of the righteous and **2.** the resurrection of the *un*righteous. The former is called "the first resurrection" in Scripture (Revelation 20:5-6), which makes the latter the second resurrection.

The second resurrection takes place at the time of the Great White Throne Judgment, detailed here:

> Then I saw a <u>great white throne</u> and him
> who was seated on it. The earth and the heavens
> fled from his presence, and there was no place
> for them. (12) And I saw the dead, great and
> small, standing before the throne, and books
> were opened. Another book was opened, which is
> the book of life. The dead were judged according
> to what they had done as recorded in the books.
> (13) The sea gave up the dead that were in it, and
> <u>death and Hades gave up</u> <u>the dead</u> <u>that were in</u>
> <u>them, and each person was judged according to</u>
> <u>what they had done.</u> (14) Then death and Hades
> were thrown into the lake of fire. The lake of fire
> is the second death. (15) <u>Anyone whose name</u>
> <u>was not found written in the book of life was</u>
> <u>thrown into the lake of fire.</u>
>
> **Revelation 20:11-15**

This massive resurrection and judgment concerns every dead soul contained in Hades (Sheol) after the thousand-year reign of Christ on this earth, which means it involves every unredeemed person throughout history. It does not include Old Testament holy people because they had a covenant with the LORD and will be resurrected after the 7-year Tribulation and before the Millennium (Matthew 19:28-30 & Daniel 12:1-2).

We'll examine the judgment of these people in the forthcoming section on the sixth basic doctrine: eternal judgment.

The Resurrection of the Righteous

The first resurrection is the resurrection of the righteous, meaning those in right-standing with God. Again, when Jesus and Paul spoke of two basic resurrections they were talking about *types* of resurrections and not numbers. While there's only one resurrection of the *un*righteous, the resurrection of the righteous takes place in *stages*, which correspond to the analogy of a harvest. In biblical times the harvest took place in three basic stages: **1.** the firstfruits, **2.** the main harvest, and **3.** the gleanings. The harvest began with the **firstfruits**, which concerned the first fruits and grains to ripen in the season and were offered to the LORD as a sacrifice of thanksgiving (Exodus 23:16,19). Later came the **general harvest** (Exodus 23:16) and, lastly, the **gleanings**, which were leftovers for the poor and needy (Leviticus 19:9-10).

Let's examine the three stages:

1. The Firstfruits. Paul described Jesus as the firstfruits here:

> But <u>Christ has indeed been raised from the dead, the firstfruits of those who have fallen asleep.</u> (21) For since death came through a man, the resurrection of the dead comes also through a man. (22) For as in Adam all die, so in Christ

all will be made alive. (23) But each in turn: <u>Christ, the firstfruits</u>; then, when he comes, those who belong to him.

1 Corinthians 15:21-23

Just as the firstfruits of the harvest were a sacrifice to the LORD so Jesus Christ was sacrificed for our sins and raised to life for our justification (Romans 4:25); hence, He's the firstfruits of the resurrection of the righteous.

2. **The General Harvest.** Verse 23 shows that the main harvest takes place when Jesus returns for the church—his "bride"—which is the Rapture, detailed in 1 Thessalonians 4:13-18. This harvest includes physically-alive believers translated to heaven.

3. **The Gleanings** refer to the righteous who were not included in the main harvest and are, as such, "leftovers." This resurrection takes place at the time of Jesus' return at the end of the Tribulation. Jesus' return to earth to establish His millennial reign is separate from the Rapture, which is when the general harvest occurs. Remember, when Jesus comes for his church he doesn't return to earth, but rather meets believers in the sky (1 Thessalonians 4:17). We'll address this in a forthcoming section. The gleanings include the resurrection of Old Testament saints—at least a bodily resurrection, but more likely a soulish/bodily resurrection—as well as the bodily resurrection of believers who died during the Tribulation.

The "gleanings" will also include believers who physically die during the Millennium. Some argue that such a resurrection won't be necessary because, as Isaiah 65:19-25 shows, lifespans will return to the lengthy durations of people before the flood, like Adam and Methuselah. However, this passage doesn't actually say righteous people *won't* die during the Millennium; notice what it says:

> **Never again will there be in it** [Jerusalem]
> **an infant who lives but a few days, or <u>an old man</u>**
> **<u>who does not live out his years</u>; <u>the one who dies</u>**
> **<u>at a hundred will be thought a mere child</u>; <u>the</u>**
> **<u>one who fails to reach a hundred</u> will be**
> **considered accursed.**
>
> **Isaiah 65:20**

The passage simply shows that lifespans will be greatly increased, as before the flood; it doesn't say righteous people won't die. In fact, it's implied that blessed people will die by the reference to "an old man who *does not live out his years*." Moreover, verse 22 says that God's people will live as long as trees during the Millennium. Depending on the species, trees can live less than a hundred years or up to a few thousand, but they ultimately die.

Something else to consider: While it's true that many people lived to be over 900 years old before the flood, it's still not a thousand years, which is how long the Millennium will last. Also, some people died well short of 900-plus years; for instance, Lamech died at 777.

Someone might argue: How can *both* the resurrection of the righteous at the beginning of the Millennium and another resurrection at the end be considered "gleanings" since they're separated by a thousand years? Answer: Because the very word "gleanings" implies more than one gleaning; after all, the poor gleaned the harvested fields more than once in biblical times. Also, Psalm 90:4 and 2 Peter 3:8 show that a thousand years is like a day to the LORD, so the two gleanings occur only one day apart from the Divine perspective.

Why is it called the "First Resurrection"?

The resurrection of the righteous is called the "first resurrection" in this passage:

> **I saw thrones on which were seated those who had been given authority to judge. And I saw the souls of those who had been beheaded because of their testimony about Jesus and because of the word of God. They had not worshiped the beast or its image and had not received its mark on their foreheads or their hands. They came to life and reigned with Christ a thousand years. (5) (The rest of the dead did not come to life until the thousand years were ended.) This is <u>the first resurrection</u>. (6) Blessed and holy are those who share in <u>the first resurrection</u>. The second death has no power over them, but they will be priests of God and of Christ and will reign with him for a thousand years.**
>
> **Revelation 20:4-6**

The passage refers specifically to the bodily resurrection of Christian martyrs from the Tribulation, which John calls the "first resurrection." By calling it the *first* resurrection is he saying that there were no resurrections before this? No, because Jesus Christ was resurrected at the beginning of the Church Age and believers will be resurrected bodily at the time of the Rapture while living believers will be translated; not to mention the resurrections of Enoch, Elijah and Moses as *types*, covered in <u>Chapter Nine</u> of *Sheol Know*. Speaking of those three, their resurrections can be considered "taste-testing of the fruit" according to the harvest analogy.

Here's a diagram that helps visualize the first and second resurrections and the three stages of the first:

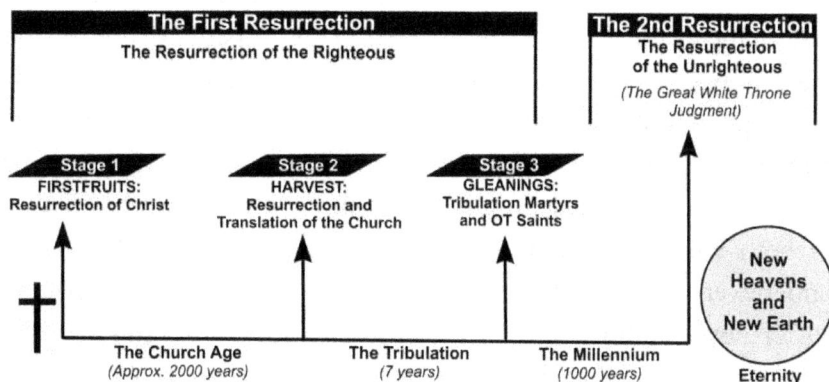

The First Resurrection
The Resurrection of the Righteous

The 2nd Resurrection
The Resurrection
of the Unrighteous
(The Great White Throne Judgment)

Stage 1	Stage 2	Stage 3
FIRSTFRUITS: Resurrection of Christ	HARVEST: Resurrection and Translation of the Church	GLEANINGS: Tribulation Martyrs and OT Saints

New Heavens and New Earth

The Church Age
(Approx. 2000 years)

The Tribulation
(7 years)

The Millennium
(1000 years)

Eternity

By calling the resurrection of the righteous the "first resurrection" John may mean more than just first in order. The Greek word for "first" is *prótos (PRO-toss)*, which also means principle, chief, honorable or most important. How is the resurrection of the righteous the more honorable resurrection? Because it entails the resurrection of people in right-standing with the LORD through covenant and spiritual rebirth (Titus 3:5 & Ephesians 4:22-24). Since this resurrection involves people who are in right-standing with their Creator, i.e. God's children, it's the more honorable resurrection and therefore the more important one to the LORD, just as the resurrection of your child would be more important to you than some stranger you never knew.

Someone might argue that all people are God's children, even atheists. No, all people are *creations* of God, but only those born-again of the seed (sperm) of Jesus Christ by the Holy Spirit are *children* of God (1 John 3:9 & 1 Peter 1:23). Because of the death and resurrection of the Messiah, Old Testament saints who were in covenant with God automatically become spiritually-regenerated at the time of their resurrection.

'Isn't this Too Complicated?'

Some might argue that the resurrection of the righteous, as just mapped out, is too complicated. This is perhaps one of the main reasons why the so-called "father of orthodoxy," Augustine of Hippo, simplified human eschatology by inventing (or, at least, popularizing) the false doctrine of amillennialism. Believe it or not, this erroneous teaching suggests that we're currently *already* in both the Millennium and Tribulation; and when believers or unbelievers die their immortal souls either go to heaven forever or suffer never-ending torment in hell. Incredibly, Augustine argued that biblical references to the new Jerusalem, new earth, new heavens and the believer's new glorified body are all symbolic language for heaven! Talk about adding to and taking away from the Holy Scriptures, a practice repeatedly denounced in the Bible (see Revelation 22:18-19, Proverbs 30:6 and Deuteronomy 4:2).[22]

Getting back to our question: Is the resurrection of the dead too complicated? Think about it like this: When referencing a complex subject to someone who knows little about the topic it's best to state the facts in the simplest of terms, which is how Jesus and Paul talked about the resurrection of the dead in John 5:28-29 and Acts 24:15 (both cited earlier). Daniel did the same thing in Daniel 12:1-2. All three of these passages detail that there will be a resurrection of both the righteous and the unrighteous, which is true, but they don't go any further than this. As such, we have to look to the rest of Scripture for more details and that's what we're doing here. This is in line with the hermeneutical rule "Scripture interprets Scripture" wherein the more clear and detailed passages offer necessary data that helps interpret the more ambiguous and sketchy ones.

---

[22] See *Hell Know* for more information on Augustine and his false doctrines that corrupted the church, specifically <u>Chapter Seven</u>'s *The Augustinian Corruption of Christendom* and <u>Chapter Nine</u>'s *The Good and Bad of Orthodoxy and Traditionalism*.

Furthermore, the argument that "this is just too complicated" implies that truth—reality—must always be simple when this simply isn't the case. Take brain surgery, for example. Is it simple or does it take years of schooling to master? How about computer technology, astronomy, world history, languages or law? How simple is the sewage system of any major city? How about the electrical grid of New York City? I could go on and on.

Yes, the resurrection of the dead is more complicated than what Augustine taught, but it's certainly not too complicated for the average person to grasp. The above diagram illustrates that it's actually not that complicated and it's much less complicated than any of the topics just listed.

As already established, the resurrection of the dead is one of the six basic doctrines (Hebrews 6:1-2). The writer of Hebrews was lamenting that the people he was addressing needed to be taught these basic doctrines all over again when they should've been teachers by this point (Hebrews 5:11-12). Now, think about it: If the topic of the resurrection of the dead was as simple as Augustine taught—that is, people just go to heaven or hell when they die to spend eternity in either bliss or torment—why would these people need to be taught the subject again? If the subject were that simplistic it'd take just a few minutes to teach and not a whole sermon or series of sermons. Moreover, if it were that simple how could the believers *not* grasp it the first time around?

Yes, the resurrection of the dead is a complicated subject, so what? That's why it needs taught properly and thoroughly.

Jesus' Rapture of His Church and His Return to Earth

I pointed out something earlier that should be elaborated on: Most believers don't realize that there are two phases to the Lord's Second Coming: **1.** Jesus' return for his Church, known as the Rapture, and **2.** Jesus' return to the earth to establish his millennial kingdom. The former is detailed in 1 Thessalonians 4:13-18 and the latter in Revelation 19:11-16. A comparison of these passages and other pertinent Scriptures reveal **two separate phases** of Jesus' Second Coming that can be distinguished like so:

The Lord's Second Coming	
PHASE 1 **The Rapture** **(1 Thessalonians 4:13-18)**	**PHASE 2** **Jesus' Return to the Earth** **(Revelation 19:11-16)**
Jesus appears in the air	Jesus returns to the earth
Jesus returns in secret, like a thief	Jesus returns openly
Jesus returns *for* his Church	Jesus returns *with* his Church
Jesus comes as Bridegroom	Jesus comes as King
Jesus comes as deliverer	Jesus comes as warrior and judge
Jesus comes with grace	Jesus comes with wrath and grace
Jesus delivers the Church *from* wrath	Jesus delivers believers (of the Tribulation) who endured wrath
Living believers receive immortal bodies as they are taken to heaven	Living believers remain mortal on the earth during the Millennium
The world is left unjudged	The world is judged (Mt. 25:31-46)
The world continues in sin	Righteousness is established
Addresses only the saved	Addresses the saved and unsaved
Can happen at any moment	Many signs must first occur
The devil continues his evil reign	The devil is cast into the Abyss

One of the differences on the list is that the Lord's return for his Church—the Rapture—can happen at any time once the general season of the end is apparent, meaning it's *imminent*, whereas many distinct signs *precede* Christ's return to the earth. These signs include, amongst others: the global cataclysm of the Tribulation period itself (Revelation 6-19), the revealing of the antichrist (2 Thessalonians 2:1-8), the two witnesses (Revelation 11:1-12) and the institution of the mark of the beast (Revelation

13:16-17). Generally speaking, once the Tribulation begins—and it will be obvious when it does—you can be sure that Jesus will return to the earth seven years later (which is different than saying you'll be able to pinpoint the precise moment or day).

However, this isn't the case with the Lord's return for his Church because, again, it's imminent and could happen at any time with zero warning once the general season of his return is at hand, which means **now** (Matthew 24:3-14). Notice what Jesus said:

> **(36) "But <u>about that day or hour no one knows, not even the angels in heaven, nor the Son, but only the Father</u>. (37) As it was in the days of Noah, so it will be at the coming of the Son of Man...**
>
> **(42) "Therefore <u>keep watch</u>, because <u>you do not know on what day your Lord will come</u>. (43) But understand this: If the owner of the house had known at what time of night the thief was coming, he would have kept watch and would not have let his house be broken into. (44) So you also must <u>be ready</u>, because <u>the Son of Man will come at an hour when you do not expect him</u>.**
>
> **Matthew 24:36-37, 42-44**

As you can see, we are instructed to "keep watch" and "be ready" because Jesus "will come at an hour when we do not expect him." Interestingly, the Son doesn't even know the day or hour, only the Father knows (verse 36). We must be "dressed ready for service" and "keep our lamps burning" (Luke 12:35) precisely because the Lord's return for his Church is imminent. I should add that, while we don't know the day or hour, we can know the general season via Jesus' descriptions and, again, that season is *now*.

While some claim that the word "Rapture" isn't biblical, it is. It refers to a phrase used in this passage:

> **After that, we who are still alive and are left will be <u>caught up</u> together with them in the clouds to meet the Lord in the air. And so we will be with the Lord forever.**
>
> **1 Thessalonians 4:17**

'Caught up' in the Greek is *harpazó (har-PAD-zoh)*, which means to "snatch up" or "obtain by robbery." It's translated in Latin as "rapio" in the Vulgate, which is where we get the English "Rapture." With this understanding, when the Bridegroom, Jesus, comes for his bride, the Church, he's going to obtain us by **robbing us off the earth!**

The aforementioned 1 Thessalonians 4:13-18 is the most prominent support text for the Rapture:

> **Brothers and sisters, we do not want you to be uninformed about those who sleep in death, so that you do not grieve like the rest of mankind, who have no hope. (14) For we believe that Jesus died and rose again, and so we believe that God will bring with Jesus those who have fallen asleep in him. (15) According to the Lord's word, we tell you that we who are still alive, who are left until the coming of the Lord, will certainly not precede those who have fallen asleep. (16) For the Lord himself will come down from heaven, with a loud command, with the voice of the archangel and with the trumpet call of God, and the dead in Christ will rise first. (17) After that, <u>we who are still alive and are left will be caught up together with them in the clouds to</u>**

meet the Lord in the air. And so we will be with the Lord forever. (18) Therefore encourage each other with these words.

1 Thessalonians 4:13-18

Here's more support:

"Do not let your hearts be troubled. You believe in God; believe also in me. (2) My Father's house has many rooms; if that were not so, would I have told you that I am going there to prepare a place for you? (3) And if I go and prepare a place for you, I will come back and take you to be with me that you also may be where I am."

John 14:1-3

Listen, I tell you a mystery: We will not all sleep, but we will all be changed—(52) in a flash, in the twinkling of an eye, at the last trumpet. For the trumpet will sound, the dead will be raised imperishable, and we will be changed.

1 Corinthians 15:51-52

and to wait for his Son from heaven, whom he raised from the dead—Jesus, who rescues us from the coming wrath.

1 Thessalonians 1:10

What is the "coming wrath" and how does Jesus "rescue" us from it? The coming wrath refers to the Tribulation and the Lord rescues the Church from it via the Rapture.

Notice what Jesus promises the faithful church of Philadelphia:

> **"Since you have kept my command to endure patiently, <u>I will also keep you from the hour of trial that is going to come on the whole world to test the inhabitants of the earth</u>."**
> **Revelation 3:10**

"The hour of trial that is going to come on the whole world" is referring to the Tribulation period detailed in Revelation 6-19. Jesus doesn't say he would just protect believers during the Tribulation, but that he'd "keep them from the hour of trial" altogether. Keep in mind that, while the church at Philadelphia was one of seven first century churches that Jesus addresses in Revelation 2-3, these seven churches were picked by the Lord because they typify the seven kinds of churches that exist throughout the Church Age. As such, Jesus' words were to all faithful Christians throughout the ensuing centuries of the Church Age. In fact, since the Rapture and the Tribulation didn't come at the general time of this message to the church of Philadelphia circa 90-100 AD, the passage *must* more specifically refer to a future generation of faithful believers.

Further support for the Rapture can be observed in what happens to John in the book of Revelation. Jesus gave John the threefold *contents* of Revelation at the end of chapter 1: "Write, therefore, **what you have seen**, **what is now** and **what will take place later**" (Revelation 1:19). This is the Contents Page of the book of Revelation: "What you have seen" refers to chapter 1 because that's what John had seen up to that point in the vision while "what is now" refers to chapters 2-3 and "what will take place later" refers to chapters 4-22.

Chapters 2-3 of Revelation cover "what is now," meaning the Church Age, as noted above. These chapters cover the seven types of churches that exist throughout the Church Age. Chapters 4-22 address "what will take place later" and chapters 4-19 specifically the period of the Tribulation, which involves the seal, trumpet and bowl judgments of God's wrath that will befall the earth and its inhabitants.

Here's my point: John was an apostle of the church and right at the beginning of Revelation 4—the beginning of his coverage of the Tribulation—Jesus says to him, "Come up here," referring to heaven (verse 1). You see? John is representative of the church and just before the Tribulation he is taken up into heaven. Why? Because the church itself will be delivered from the Tribulation via Jesus' return for his church, which is the Rapture.

Another thing to consider is that the church is referred to no less than nineteen times in the first three chapters of Revelation and not once on earth in chapters 4-19. Why? Because the existing church—all genuine believers—will be "snatched up" to heaven before the Tribulation starts. Revelation 19 details Christ's return to the earth at the end of the Tribulation. Guess who's riding with him? The church (verse 14; also verified by 1 Thessalonians 4:14).

This doesn't mean, however, that there won't be believers during the Tribulation because there will be multitudes; and, yes, they *are* the church because 'church' simply refers to the *ekklesia (ek-klay-SEE-ah)*, the "called-out ones" who are called out of the darkness of this world into the kingdom of light. However, the *existing church* at the time of the Rapture before the Tribulation will have been snatched away. In other words, believers *during* the Tribulation embraced the gospel *after* the Rapture. We'll address this in the next section.

The snatching up of the church before the Tribulation corresponds to the biblical pattern of the righteous being saved from destruction when God's judgment falls on unrepentant masses. Jesus noted this pattern when he taught on the Rapture:

For the Son of Man <u>in his day will be like</u> <u>the lightning, which flashes and lights up the sky</u> <u>from one end to the other</u>. (25) But first he must suffer many things and be rejected by this generation.

(26) "<u>Just as it was in the days of Noah, so</u> <u>also will it be</u> in the days of the Son of Man. (27) People were eating, drinking, marrying and being given in marriage up to the day Noah entered the ark. Then the flood came and destroyed them all.

(28) "<u>It was the same in the days of Lot.</u> People were eating and drinking, buying and selling, planting and building. (29) But the day Lot left Sodom, fire and sulfur rained down from heaven and destroyed them all.

(30) "It will be just like this <u>on the day the</u> <u>Son of Man is revealed</u>. (31) On that day no one who is on the housetop, with possessions inside, should go down to get them. Likewise, no one in the field should go back for anything. (32) Remember Lot's wife! (33) Whoever tries to keep their life will lose it, and whoever loses their life will preserve it. (34) I tell you, <u>on that night</u> <u>two people will be in one bed; one will be taken</u> <u>and the other left</u>. (35) <u>Two women will be</u> <u>grinding grain together; one will be taken and</u> <u>the other left</u>."

Luke 17:24-35

Jesus is talking about "the day the Son of Man is revealed" (verse 30) that "will be like the lightning, which flashes and lights up the sky from one end to the other" (verse 24). In other words, it'll take place in the blink of an eye. The last two verses show beyond any shadow of doubt that Jesus was talking about His snatching up of the church: "Two people will be in bed; one will be taken and the other left. Two women will be grinding grain together; one will be taken and the other left" (verses 34-35). This, incidentally, presents a problem for those who argue that the Rapture takes place at the same time as Jesus' return to the earth at the end of the Tribulation because the impression of these verses is that of ordinary every-day life and not of people who just went through a worldwide cataclysm horrifically described in Revelation 6-19.

Observe in verses 26-29 how Jesus likens the time of the Rapture to the "days of Noah" and the "days of Lot." "Just as it was" in the days of these two "so it will be" when Christ returns for his church. What's the significance of this? In the days of Noah and Lot there were warnings of the LORD's coming judgment on masses of people if they stubbornly refused to repent. In Noah's situation the judgment concerned the entire world whereas in Lot's situation it concerned the cities of Sodom and Gomorrah. In both cases **the righteous were removed *before* God's judgment fell**. "So it will be" with the future Tribulation—those in right-standing with God will be taken out of the way *before* His wrath falls on rebellious humanity. Those who become believers during the Tribulation are those who wisely respond to the pouring out of God's wrath by repenting.

In verse 30 Jesus says "It will be just like this on the day the Son of Man is revealed." Just like what? Just like the days of Noah and Lot where people were carrying on business as usual— eating, drinking, marrying, buying, selling, planting and building (verses 27-28). This is what people will be doing when Jesus comes for his church, not enduring a global upheaval, which disproves the post-Tribulation position.

Speaking of the post-Tribulation view, how do people who hold this position explain Luke 17:24-35? They argue that Jesus only speaks of his coming *once* in this passage, not twice, and when he comes he will **1.** snatch up the righteous and then **2.** pour out his wrath on the unrighteous, citing verses 26-32. The problem with this, of course, is that *it's an explicit description of the pre-Tribulation position* (or, at least, "pre-wrath"). The only thing they're omitting is Jesus' return to the earth *after* God's wrath is poured out on rebellious humanity to set up his millennial kingdom (Matthew 25:31). As already explained, this is detailed in the book of Revelation: In Revelation 4:1 Jesus says to John—representing the church—to "come up here" to heaven. Chapters 4-19 cover the Tribulation where God's wrath is poured out and Jesus returns to the earth at the end (Revelation 19).

Here's a timeline diagram to help visualize these events:

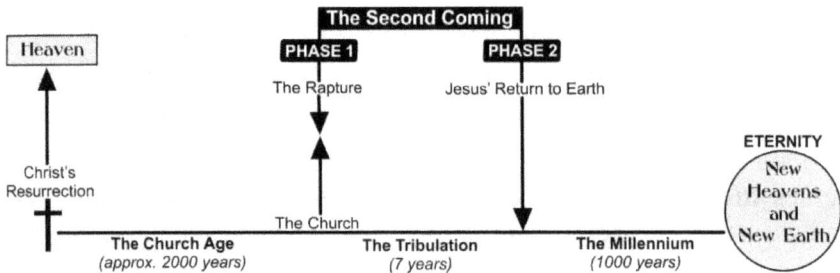

Some people suggest that the Rapture isn't part of Jesus' Second Coming and that only His return to the earth should be designated as the Second coming, but Jesus himself spoke of his snatching up of the church as **"the coming of the Son of Man"** (Matthew 24:27,37,39) and within this context are clear references to the Tribulation (verses 21-22 & 29). The Greek for "coming" in these passages is *parousia (par-oo-SEE-ah)*, traditionally translated as "advent" in Christian circles as in "the Second Advent of Christ." This is the same word used to describe the Lord's coming at the *end* of the Tribulation in 2 Thessalonians 2:8. Jesus elsewhere referred to this latter coming as **"When the Son of Man comes** in his glory" (Matthew 16:27 & 25:31). Since the Rapture of the church is clearly separate from the Lord's coming to the earth—with the Tribulation separating them—and both the Rapture and Jesus' return to the earth are described in terms of "coming" then we must conclude that **they both represent his Second Coming**, albeit two phases.

Someone might argue: "But these two phases are separated by several years, how can they both refer to the *same* Second Coming? Because it's *one* coming taking place in *two* stages. Besides, seven years isn't that long of a time to the eternal God. Let me put it in perspective: The Bible says that a thousand years is like a day to the Lord (Psalm 90:4 & 2 Peter 3:8), which means that seven years would be like 10½ minutes! So from Jesus' perspective the Second Coming—both stages—takes place in 10½ minutes. It's hard to get out of the airport without baggage in that amount of time!

"For it will Not be, Unless <u>the Departure</u> Comes First"

Both phases of the Lord's Second Coming are covered in this passage:

> **Now, brothers, <u>concerning the coming of our Lord Jesus Christ</u>, <u>and our gathering together to him</u>, we ask you (2) not to be quickly shaken in your mind, nor yet be troubled, either by spirit, or by word, or by letter as from us, saying that <u>the day of Christ</u> had come. (3) Let no one deceive you in any way. <u>For it will not be, unless the departure comes first, and the man of sin is revealed</u>, the son of destruction, (4) who opposes and exalts himself against all that is called God or that is worshiped; so that he sits as**

God in the temple of God, setting himself up as God. (5) Don't you remember that, when I was still with you, I told you these things? (6) <u>Now you know what is restraining him</u>, to the end that he may be revealed in his own season. (7) For the mystery of lawlessness already works. <u>Only there is one who restrains now, until he is taken out of the way.</u> (8) <u>Then the lawless one will be revealed</u>, whom <u>the Lord will kill with the breath of his mouth, and destroy by the manifestation of his coming</u>;

2 Thessalonians 2:1-8 (WEB)

Verse 1 shows that this text concerns the Second Coming, including the church being "gathered together to him," which is the Rapture. Verse 8 details the second phase of Jesus' coming, which is when he returns to the earth and destroys the "lawless one"—the antichrist—with a mere word or two from his lips. (So much for Christ being a milksop weakling as he's often maligned in modern Western culture!) The Greek word for "coming" in both verses is the aforementioned *parousia*. You see? The Second Coming consists of **1.** Jesus' return for his church and **2.** His return to the earth to vanquish his enemies and establish his millennial kingdom.

Verse 3 reveals the sequence of events, emphasizing that the "day of Christ" will not come to pass *until* "the departure comes first, and the man of sin is revealed." The "departure" is an obvious reference to the snatching up of the church while the revealing of the "man of sin" refers to the unveiling of the antichrist, a wicked, possessed man who will obtain worldwide power during the Tribulation (Revelation 13:7).

The Greek word for "departure" is *apostasia (ap-os-tas-EE-ah)* and is only used one other time in the Bible where it refers to departing from the law of Moses (Acts 21:21). Interestingly, the word was translated as "departure" or "departing" in 2 Thessalonians 2:3 in the first seven English translations of the Bible, which changed when the King James translators decided to translate it as "falling away." Most modern English versions have followed suit by translating it as "apostasy" or "rebellion," but the World English Bible (above) translates it as "departure." I believe this is the proper translation for a few reasons:

1. The verb form of the word is used 14 times in the New Testament where it predominantly means "departed." Luke 2:37 is a good example where it refers to an elderly prophetess who "never *left* the temple but worshiped night and day, fasting and praying;" Acts 12:10 is another example where it refers to an angel *leaving* Peter after helping him escape from prison.

2. It doesn't make sense in the context of 2 Thessalonians 2:3 to translate *apostasia* as "rebellion" or "apostasy"/"falling away." Concerning the former, the world has always been in rebellion against genuine Christianity (please notice I said "genuine"). Concerning the latter, there's *already* mass apostasy in Christendom with whole denominations embracing gross libertinism and rejecting the most obvious biblical axioms. In fact, this has been increasing for *decades*.

3. Translating *apostasia* as "departure" fits both the immediate context of 2 Thessalonians 2:1-8 and the greater context of the Lord's Second Coming in the Bible, the latter of which we've already covered. Concerning the former, verse 1 speaks of the Second Coming in terms of the church being gathered to Jesus, which involves believers *departing* from this earth. And verses 6-8 speak of the "restrainer" of lawlessness, which must be **removed** *before* the antichrist can rise to power. Who is this "restrainer" of lawlessness? The most obvious answer is the

Holy Spirit and, by extension, the church, which is the temple of the Holy Spirit (1 Corinthians 3:16). When they depart the earth the antichrist will no longer be restrained and, in the vacuum, he will make his move. Whereas the church will remain in heaven during the Tribulation the Holy Spirit will return as masses of wise people will almost immediately turn to God after the incredible testimony of the Rapture. The Holy Spirit obviously returns because it's the Spirit who regenerates people through the gospel (Titus 3:5). As noted earlier, untold millions will be saved during the Tribulation (Revelation 7:9,14) through the testimony of **1.** the Rapture, **2.** the 144,000 Jewish evangelists, **3.** the two witnesses, **4.** the mass divine judgments, and **5.** an angel commissioned to preach the eternal gospel to the inhabitants of the earth (Revelation 14:6-7).

As you can see, 2 Thessalonians 2:1-8 strongly supports the two phases of the Second Coming and the pre-Tribulation Rapture.

Let me close by stressing that I personally don't care if the Rapture takes place before the Tribulation, mid-Tribulation or "pre-wrath." I don't even care if it takes place at the same general time as Jesus' return to the earth at the end of the Tribulation. Don't get me wrong, like any sane believer I have zero desire to go through the Tribulation, but as a responsible minister of the Word of God all I care about is accurately conveying what the Bible teaches and my studies have led me to conclude what is contained in these last two sections. Bear in mind that I'm a devoted non-sectarian and therefore don't draw doctrinal conclusions based on the pressure of a certain group. I draw conclusions from the God-breathed Scriptures and, as you see, they overwhelmingly point in the direction of a pre-Tribulation Rapture.

I encourage you to unbiasedly look at the different perspectives in your studies and draw your own conclusions with the help of the Holy Spirit. I recommend the works of David Reagan, Hal Lindsey and Todd Strandberg.

Lastly, all genuine believers who know how to read agree that the Lord will "snatch up" his church when he returns based on the clear passages we've looked at in this section, so the Rapture is a biblical fact. It's the *timing* of the Rapture that believers disagree on and this is a secondary issue; it's not something to argue about or break fellowship over. Whether pre, mid, post or pre-wrath, the Rapture *will* occur.

6. Eternal Judgment

The sixth basic doctrine of Christianity is that all persons will stand before God and the judgment will have eternal ramifications. The word "eternal" in the Greek is the adjective *aionios (aay-OH-nee-us)*, which is derived from *aion (aay-OHN)*. *Aion* is where we get the English 'eon,' meaning "an age." As such, *aionios* means "like an age" or "age-lasting." Since *aionios* in the phrase "eternal judgment" refers to the coming age of the new heavens and new earth, which is an everlasting age, God's judgment on people at the end of this current age relates to the coming eternal age. Are you with me?

Notice how this verse describes God:

> **There is only one Lawgiver and Judge,**
> **the one who is able to <u>save</u> and <u>destroy</u>.**
> **James 4:12**

This is a New Testament passage and it describes the LORD in terms of being a Judge, a Judge who's going to do one of two things with people depending on what they choose to do or not do on earth: He's either going to **save** or **destroy**. Whether salvation or destruction, the judgment is eternal, meaning it applies to the never-ending age to come, which is the age of the new heavens and new earth (2 Peter 3:7,13).

There are four judgments and they apply to the unrighteous (i.e. the lost), the righteous in Christ, and Old Testament saints. I share them in this order because that's the order we're going to look at them.

The Great White Throne Judgment: Eternal Judgment of the Lost

The eternal judgment of the unredeemed is solemnly detailed in this passage:

> **(13) The sea gave up the dead that were in it, and death and Hades gave up the dead that were in them, and each person was judged according to what they had done. (14) Then death and Hades were thrown into the lake of fire. <u>The lake of fire is the second death</u>. (15) <u>Anyone whose name was not found written in the book of life was thrown into the lake of fire</u>.**
>
> **Revelation 20:13-15**

God's judgment for anyone whose name is not found written in the book of life is being cast into the lake of fire, which is described as the "second death." This is the judgment of the unrepentant wicked spoken of in Hebrews in terms of "raging fire that will *consume* the enemies of God" (Hebrews 10:26-27).

Paul described the second death as "everlasting destruction" (2 Thessalonians 1:9) while Jesus was even more explicit:

> **"Do not be afraid of those who kill the body but cannot kill the soul. Rather, be afraid of the One [God] who can <u>destroy both soul and body in hell</u>** *(Gehenna)."*
>
> **Matthew 10:28**

God's going to literally destroy the unrepentant wicked in the lake of fire, not preserve them for eternal roasting torture. Jesus elsewhere described human damnation in terms of "eternal punishment" (Matthew 25:46) but there's a difference between eternal punishment and eternal punish*ing*. The Greek word for "punishment" is *kolasis (KOL-as-is),* which refers to a "penal infliction" and is therefore a judicial sentence. Jesus does not say in Matthew 25 what the penal infliction will be, only that it will take place in the lake of fire ("the eternal fire") and that this infliction will last forever (that is, take place in the age to come, which lasts forever). Since Jesus doesn't specify what exactly the penal sentence is, we must therefore turn to the rest of Scripture for answers. "Scripture interprets Scripture" is an interpretational rule. And we see above that Jesus plainly said God would "**destroy** both soul and body" in the lake of fire.

For additional evidence, consider these four points that reinforce each other:

1. Jesus and the apostles plainly taught what would happen to ungodly people when they suffer "the second death." They taught that:

   - the ungodly would **die** (John 11:26 & Romans 8:13),
   - that they would experience **death** (John 8:51, Romans 6:23 & James 5:20),
   - that **destruction** would occur (Matthew 7:13 & 2 Peter 3:7),

- that both their souls and bodies would be **destroyed** (Matthew 10:28 & James 4:12),
- and that they would **perish** (John 3:16 & 2 Peter 3:9).

As you can see, the Bible continually speaks of the eternal fate of the unrepentant wicked in explicit terms of destruction: "die," "death," "destruction," "destroy" and "perish." I refer to this as the "language of destruction." The Holy Spirit wrote the Scriptures via men of God (2 Peter 1:20-21) and the terminology the Holy Spirit chose to use was the language of destruction, not the language of eternal conscious torture.

2. In a desperate effort to repudiate the above, advocates of eternal torture try to claim that the Greek word translated as "destroy" and "perish" in passages like Matthew 10:28 and John 3:16—*apollumi (ah-POHL-loo-mee)*—means "destruc-tion, not of being, but of well-being." However this is easily disproven because Jesus used this very word (as conveyed by Luke) to describe the incineration of the people of Sodom (Luke 17:29). Bear in mind that both the Old and New Testaments detail that Sodom & Gomorrah were **burned to ashes** and, even more, that this total incineration is **an example of what will happen to the ungodly** on the day of judgment (2 Peter 2:6). What word did Christ use to describe this incineration in Luke 17:29? Why, *appolumi*, the very same word translated as "destroy" in Matthew 10:28 and "perish" in John 3:16. Enough said.

3. Backing up the above two points are the unmistakable **examples** of literal destruction used in reference to the second death, like weeds thrown into fire and burned (Matthew 13:40). Tell me, what happens to weeds cast into fire? Do they burn forever and ever without ever quite burning up or do they burn for a little while, but ultimately **burn up**? ("Burn up" is incidentally the way John the Baptist described human damnation in Matthew 3:12 and Luke 3:17). Then there's

Jesus' example of the enemies of the king (figurative of Christ) being brought before him and **executed** in front of him, not preserved and perpetually tormented in his presence (Luke 19:27). Another great example is that of "hell" itself. The only Greek word translated as "hell" in English Bibles is *Gehenna*, which literally means Valley of Hinnom or Hinnom Valley. This ravine was a trash dump and incinerator located outside the southwest walls of Jerusalem at the time of Christ. You can see it on close-up maps of Jerusalem in the backs of most Bibles. Jesus used *Gehenna* as a figure for the lake of fire and human damnation that his listeners readily understood. Trash and carcasses of animals and despised criminals weren't thrown into Gehenna to be preserved, but rather to be discarded and eradicated. It's the same with the unrighteous on Judgment Day when they're cast into the lake of fire.

4. The above points are further reinforced by the fact that **eternal life and immortality are only available to people through the gospel of Christ**, as clearly shown in 2 Timothy 1:10 and Romans 2:7. Jesus plainly said that human beings are mortal apart from redemption and that angelic spirits possess intrinsic immortality, even wicked spirits (Luke 20:34-36), which explains why the lake of fire—the "eternal fire"—was "prepared for the devil and his angels" as their eternal habitation (Matthew 25:41). However, human beings are mortal apart from redemption in Christ. The very reason the LORD was sure to banish Adam & Eve from the Garden of Eden was so that they wouldn't "eat of the tree of life and live forever" (Genesis 3:22-24) and **thus suffer the same fate as the devil and his angels**. Only the redeemed will be allowed to "eat of the tree of life" and live forever (Revelation 2:7).

For important details see both *Hell Know* and *Sheol Know* (abridged versions are available on the internet, but I recommend the published versions).

The Great White Throne Judgment brings up an obvious question: Will every person who partakes of this judgment automatically be cast into the lake of fire? After all, what about those who never heard the gospel? What about those who heard the gospel but didn't understand it for one legitimate reason or another? What about those who rejected it because it was either a flawed, religionized version of the gospel or it came with serious baggage, like imperialism? Every legitimate minister of God's Word must consider these obvious questions and try to answer them based on what the Bible says and simple common sense. I would be seriously skeptical of anyone who doesn't do this, particularly those who write off such questions in preference to the official position of whatever group they adhere to, which is an example of rigid sectarianism. Religious faction-ism like this actually hinders the truth and, in fact, is a form of legalism, i.e. counterfeit Christianity. Remember, Jesus said it's the truth that will set us free (John 8:31-32), so anything that *hinders* the acquisition of truth is not good. In any case, these questions are explored in *Hell Know*.

The Sheep and Goat Judgment

This judgment concerns non-Christians still alive on earth after God's judgment falls on humanity during the Tribulation, detailed in Revelation 6-19. When the mighty conqueror Jesus Christ returns to earth to set up His millennial kingdom He will judge the living nations, as shown in Matthew 25:31-46. They will be judged according to how they treat Tribulation saints—people who embrace the gospel during the Tribulation due to the testimony of **1.** the Rapture of the church (1 Thessalonians 4:13-18), **2.** the 144,000 Jewish evangelists, **3.** the two witnesses, **4.** the mass divine judgments, and **5.** an angel commissioned to preach the eternal gospel to the inhabitants of the earth (Revelation 14:6-7). These believers will be greatly persecuted during the antichrist's worldwide reign of terror. The living nations will be judged according to how they treat these Tribulation saints. Those who had regard for believers—the body of Christ—and acted accordingly will be designated as "sheep," promised eternal life, and allowed to enter the Millennium as mortals whereas those who disregard and persecute believers will be cast into the lake of fire, God's trash dump, to suffer the second death.

You can read more about these events in *Sheol Know* Chapter Eleven.

The Judgment Seat of Christ

The Judgment Seat of Christ is detailed in this passage:

> **For we must all appear before the judgment seat of Christ, so that each of us may receive what is due us for the things done while in the body, whether good or bad.**
>
> **(11) Since, then, we know what it is to fear the Lord, we try to persuade others.**
>
> **2 Corinthians 5:10-11**

Paul is addressing believers in this passage and he says that we must all appear before the Judgment Seat of Christ. This is the judgment that believers will experience and is also called the Bema *(BAY-mah)* Judgment, named after the Greek word for "judgment seat." Spiritually-regenerated Christians will not be evaluated at the Great White Throne Judgment, as that judgment only concerns spiritually-dead people (Revelation 20:11-15).

The purpose of the Judgment Seat of Christ is obviously not to determine who will be granted eternal life, as all spiritually born-again believers rightfully possess such, although there may be exceptions. The purpose of this judgment is to acknowledge and reward Christians for the good things they did while in the body and to rebuke and penalize them for the bad. The "bad" will not include sins humbly confessed because God forgives all such sins and purifies us from the corresponding unrighteousness (1 John 1:8-9). The "bad" would include both *unconfessed* sins of commission and sins of omission, as well as an appraisal of our works. A sin of commission is something that we *do,* like gossip and slander. A sin of omission involves something that we don't do that we should have done. For instance, if God prompts a lady to give someone in need $100 and she doesn't do it, or if the LORD calls a lawyer into full-time ministry and he ignores the call. These are sins of omission.

There's something in the above passage that we need to consider: After stating that Christians will receive what is due them for the good or bad things they did, the apostle Paul then says in verse 11: "Since then, we know what it is to **fear the Lord**." The King James Version translates this as "Knowing therefore **the terror of the Lord**." This statement makes no sense if people just receive *rewards* at the Judgment Seat of Christ, as I've heard some ministers erroneously teach. Knowing that Christians will be held accountable for the bad things they do in this life can inspire some healthy "terror." For those of us who are Christians, it's spiritually healthy to regularly remind ourselves that we will one day stand before the throne of God Himself and give an accounting of our lives. Needless to say, the fear of the Lord inspires holy (pure) living. It inspires humbly "keeping with repentance" when we miss it.

The Greek word for 'judgment' in reference to the sixth basic doctrine, "eternal judgment" (Hebrews 6:2), is *krima (KREE-mah)*, which means "judgment, verdict or lawsuit." The Greek for 'judgment seat' in the phrase "judgment seat of Christ" is a different word, the aforementioned *bema (BAY-mah)*, which refers to a platform or throne from which justice is administered. Because of this, some might suggest that the sixth basic doctrine—eternal judgment—doesn't apply to believers, but it does. For instance, it says in James 3:1 that "Not many of you should become teachers, my fellow believers, because you know that we who teach will be judged more strictly." James was addressing *believers* and says that those who teach will be judged more strictly. More literal translations say that those who teach will "receive a stricter judgment" (e.g. NASB and NKJV). The word "judgment" (or "judged" in the NIV) is the aforementioned *krima* used in the phrase "eternal judgment" in Hebrews 6:2. Where do you suppose those who teach God's Word will experience this stricter judgment? Not the Great White Throne Judgment, since that judgment applies strictly to spiritually unregenerated *un*believers. No, these teachers will be judged at the Judgment Seat of Christ, which is where believers are judged.

I've had ministers write me because they object to the notion of believers being judged on the grounds that Christ returns "to bring salvation to those who are waiting for him" and (supposedly) not to judge them (Hebrews 9:28). Yes, Jesus is returning to bring salvation to believers, but this does not negate the reality and necessity of the Bema Judgment, as detailed above.

I know believers who rip off people in business without a second thought or readily engage in gossip & slander, usually due to hidden (but obvious) envy, rivalry and malice. What doctrine of demons have they embraced to cause them to walk in such blatant unrighteousness without repentance? Answer: The false doctrine that believers can sin all they want with no care of repentance and never be held accountable because "Jesus is returning to bring salvation only to believers and no judgment whatsoever." It's a wicked and thoroughly unbiblical doctrine! The Judgment Seat of Christ is part of the six basic doctrines and is therefore a foundational teaching of true Christianity. It inspires God-fearing holiness and a spirit of humble repentance in believers and protects them from false doctrine, like the idea that believers won't have to stand before Christ at His Judgment Seat.

For more details on the Judgment Seat of Christ see *Hell Know* <u>Chapter Eight</u>.

The Judgment of Old Testament Saints

The sixth basic doctrine of eternal judgment applies to one final group and that's the Old Testament saints. They will be judged at the time of their resurrection when the Lord returns to the earth to establish His millennial reign, which takes place at the end of the Tribulation, as shown in the following two passages:

> **"At that time Michael, the great prince who protects <u>your people</u>, will arise. There will be <u>a time of distress such as has not happened from the beginning of nations until then</u>. But at that time <u>your people</u>—everyone whose name is found written in the book—will be delivered. (2) Multitudes who sleep in the dust of the earth will awake: some to everlasting life, others to shame and everlasting contempt."**
>
> **Daniel 12:1-2**

Daniel prophesies that the resurrection of the Israelites will not take place until after a "time of distress" so great that such a thing never occurred before in the history of humanity. This refers to the Tribulation detailed in the book of Revelation (chapters 6-19). Daniel speaks in general terms of the righteous who will be delivered or resurrected at this time. He refers to them as "your people"—i.e. God's people—and **everyone whose name is found written in the book**," which would of course include more than just Old Testament holy people; it would include Christian martyrs during the Tribulation, as well as living believers.

Jesus gets more specific about the resurrection and judgment of Old Testament saints in this passage:

> **Jesus said to them, "Truly I tell you, at the renewal of all things, when the Son of Man sits on his glorious throne, you who have followed me will also sit on twelve thrones, <u>judging the twelve tribes of Israel</u>. (29) And everyone who has left houses or brothers or sisters or father or mother or wife or children or fields for my sake will receive a hundred times as much and will inherit eternal life. (30) But many who are first will be last, and many who are last will be first."**
>
> **Matthew 19:28-30**

Some might inquire why Old Testament saints are not resurrected at the time of Jesus' return for his church—that is, the Rapture—which is when believers are either bodily resurrected or translated (1 Thessalonians 4:13-18), but this idea is negated by the obvious fact that the Rapture concerns the Lord's return for His church—His bride—and not his return for holy people of the Old Testament period.

I encourage you to master the six basic doctrines of Christianity as detailed in these last two chapters. Those who do so set a solid foundation for their spiritual walk, which protects them from false doctrine and feeble quasi-spirituality.

Chapter Eleven

How to be Spirit-Controlled

The full title of this chapter is "How to be Spirit-Controlled Rather than Flesh-ruled." A good alternative title would be "How to Walk FREE from Sin" because the way to walk free from sin and its root cause—the flesh or sinful nature—is to learn how to be spirit-controlled rather than flesh-ruled. If this doesn't make sense, it will as we progress.

There are **three things** that enable the believer to be spirit-controlled rather than flesh-ruled, and they correspond to the three parts of human nature—spirit, mind and body. You could call these the three keys to walking in the spirit. I almost didn't include this chapter because these three keys are covered to some extent in previous chapters, but decided to add it because this chapter nicely puts the three keys together in the context of walking free from sin and the flesh.

This chapter is important to me because I was once in bondage to the flesh in my youth and struggled greatly to escape it. With God's help and His Word, not to mention mighty mentors, like Joe Cameneti, I slowly learned how to walk free of the flesh and desperately want to share how I did it with anyone who needs it so they too can be free.

True Spirituality

In short, the answer to being in bondage to the flesh is **spirituality**. That might sound anticlimactic to you—even lame—but let me explain. While 'spirituality' is a term that's thrown around a lot—sometimes by people who aren't really spiritual—it actually refers to the spirit-controlled life. This merely means being spirit-driven rather than flesh-driven; it means being controlled by your higher self as opposed to the lower self. To do this you simply have to learn to put off the old self and put on the new:

> **You were taught with regard to your former way of life, to <u>put off your old self</u>, which is being corrupted by its deceitful desires; (23) to be made new in the attitude of your minds; (24) and to <u>put on the new self</u>, created to be <u>like God</u> in <u>true righteousness</u> and <u>holiness</u>.**
> **Ephesians 4:22-24**

This passage contains the antidote to walking free of the flesh. It's therefore imperative that we *get* it. The "old self" is the flesh or sin nature and we are instructed to put it off. Why? Because the old self is corrupted by "deceitful desires." Your flesh has desires, which means it has a voice, but these desires are deceitful. They promise happiness but they don't deliver. They can only ultimately bring death and all that goes with it. We are told to "put off" these fleshly desires. In the Greek this means to strip it off. We have to strip off the old way of thinking in favor of a new way. Verse 23 tells us how to do this: We must be made new in the attitude of our minds. What's the new attitude we should have? We are to count ourselves dead to the old self and alive to God in Christ Jesus (Romans 6:11). Counting ourselves alive to God includes accepting everything God says we are in Christ, that is, who we are in our new self, the spirit. We'll address this in the next section.

This results in what verse 24 calls putting "on the new self," which means living out of our spirits as led of the Holy Spirit. When we do this we'll be spirit-controlled and naturally produce the fruit thereof.

The New Testament describes this in different ways: When we are spirit-controlled we "live by the spirit" (Galatians 5:16), we "clothe ourselves with the Lord Jesus Christ" (Romans 13:14), we "participate in the divine nature" (2 Peter 1:4), we "put on the new self" (Colossians 3:10). How can putting on the new self be described as clothing ourselves with Christ or participating in the divine nature? Because the "new self" refers to our regenerated spirit which was "created to be *like God* in true righteousness and holiness" (verse 24).

If there's a *true* righteousness and holiness there's also a *false* righteousness and holiness, which is legalism. True righteousness and holiness can only be attained by, first, being born-again spiritually and, second, living out of your spirit rather than the flesh. The latter is a learning process, of course, and takes time, but the more you do it the easier it is and the more fruit you'll produce. The fruits of the spirit are the fruits of God's nature. Hence, those who live by their spirit, which is guided by the Holy Spirit, will be "like God" because the spirit naturally produces the fruits of his nature:

> **The acts of the sinful nature are obvious:**
> **sexual immorality, impurity and debauchery;**
> **(20) idolatry and witchcraft; hatred, discord,**
> **jealousy,   fits   of   rage,   selfish   ambition,**

dissensions, factions (21) and envy; drunkenness, orgies, and the like. I warn you, as I did before, that those who live like this will not inherit the kingdom of God. (22) But the fruit of the spirit is love, joy, peace, patience, kindness, goodness, faithfulness, (23) gentleness and self-control. Against such things there is no law.

Galatians 5:19-23

This list of the fruit of the spirit isn't exhaustive any more than the list of the works of the flesh is exhaustive. God has many other character traits, like righteousness (Philippians 1:11), truth (Ephesians 5:9), power (2 Timothy 1:7), righteous anger (Mark 3:1-6) and boldness (Mark 11:15-18).

The awesome news is that believers can walk free of the works of the flesh and the two ways they manifest in the church— legalism and libertinism—simply by putting off the flesh in favor of participating in the divine nature. If this weren't possible Paul would never have instructed us to "be imitators of God" in Ephesians 5:1.

Speaking of Ephesians 5:1, Christians are usually blown away by this verse. They ask, "How can *I* possibly imitate God?" It's simple: Put off the flesh and learn to live out of your spirit and you'll automatically participate in the divine nature and produce the very fruit of God's character!

So how exactly do we walk in the spirit like this? There are **three things** that we have to do and they correspond to the three parts of human nature—mind, body and spirit (I only put them in that order because we're going to look at them in that order). These are the three keys to walking in the spirit. Let's look at each key, starting with the mind.

1. Count Yourself Dead to Sin and Alive to God

The first thing you need to do in order to walk in the spirit has to do with **the mind**. Paul said that we are to be transformed by the renewing of our mind in Romans 12:2. The Greek word translated as "transformed" is where we get the English 'metamorphosis,' which means to be transformed as the result of a *process*. A great example of this would be a lowly and not-particularly-good-looking caterpillar being transformed in its cocoon and emerging as a beautiful butterfly. Think about it, caterpillars crawl on the ground and are kind of ugly, whereas butterflies are beautiful and can fly. Believers can have just as stunning a transformation, but it involves renewing the mind—we must let go of caterpillar-thinking (flesh-ruled thinking) in favor of butterfly-thinking (spirit-controlled thinking).

Here's a cornerstone passage on renewing the mind and being spirit-controlled:

> **The death he died, he died to sin once for all; but the life he lives, he lives to God.**
> **(11) In the same way, <u>count yourselves dead to sin</u> but <u>alive to God in Christ Jesus</u>. (12) Therefore do not let sin reign in your mortal body so that you obey its evil desires.**
> **Romans 6:10-12**

Verse 12 reveals the goal of this instruction—not letting sin reign in your body so that you obey its evil desires. In short, the goal is to *not* be flesh-ruled. Verse 11 shows us how to attain this goal: First, we must count ourselves dead to sin and, second, we must count ourselves alive to God in Christ Jesus.

Concerning the first part, counting ourselves dead to sin involves a new way of thinking. We must start counting ourselves as dead to the sins that normally tempt us if we want to experience freedom. For instance, if you have a weakness for lying, gossip, drunkenness or lust, you have to start making it your mindset that you are dead to these things. I used to have a problem with fits of rage so I had to start making it my mindset that I was dead to fits of rage in order to eventually walk in freedom. Making something your mindset includes making it your confession because words have the power of life and death (Proverbs 18:21). So I made this my regular confession: "I Dirk Waren am dead to fits of rage."

The second part of verse 11 is just as important. We have to count ourselves as "alive to God in Christ Jesus." Being alive to God in Christ Jesus is the opposite of being dead to God in the bondage of the flesh. So if you make it your mindset that you're dead to sin, be sure to also make it your mindset that you're alive to the opposite. For example, I made it my belief and confession that I'm dead to fits of rage, but I added that I'm alive to peace and self-control. Or say if a brother has a problem with lying or exaggeration, he would make it his mindset that he's dead to lying but alive to the truth. Or say if a sister has a problem with gossip and slander (which go hand-and-hand) she would make it her confession that she's dead to gossip and slander and alive to praying for others and blessing them.

Whatever your sin weakness is, count yourself dead to it and counteract it with the truth of *who you already are in your regenerated spirit*. You see, this whole instruction is geared to getting the believer spirit-focused instead of flesh-focused, spirit-ruled instead of flesh-ruled. For instance, the brother who has a problem with lying has a problem with lying because his flesh has a problem with lying. The only way for him to escape this condition is to stop being flesh-ruled because he'll continue to have a problem with lying as long as he's flesh-ruled. To walk free he'll have to learn to be spirit-ruled by changing his thinking so that it agrees with who he is in his spirit rather than who he is in his flesh. Remember, our regenerated spirit was "created to be like God in true righteousness and holiness" (Ephesians 4:24). If you're a believer your spirit is *already* righteous and holy; it doesn't have a sin problem like your lower nature. It's whole and complete, which is what holiness is. The key to freedom is to line up your thinking with who you are in your spirit rather than who you are in your flesh.

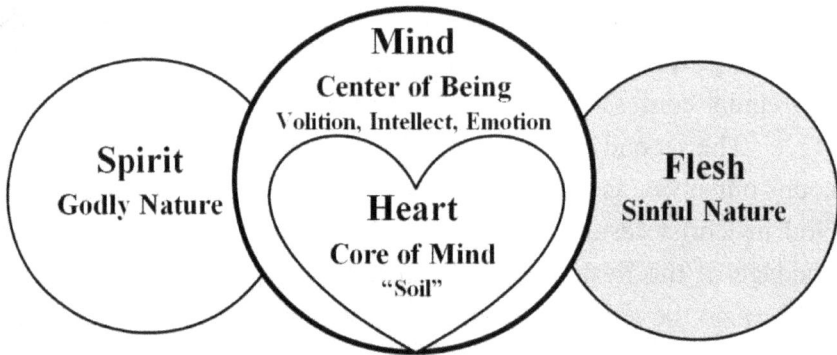

This isn't merely a "mind over matter" principle, as some might think. If you're a believer, you can genuinely count yourself dead to sin because you *are* dead to sin in your spirit. Even if you don't feel like you're dead to sin, you *are* dead to sin. It's who you already are in your spirit because *your spirit is righteous and holy like God!*

By the way, renewing your mind in this manner is tied to repentance since 'repent' literally means to change your mind for the better. Both the Greek words for 'repentance' and 'repent' are derived from the Greek word for mind, which is *nous* (*noos*). **To repent means to change your thinking, your mindset, your attitude to the positive**. Any other type of "repentance" is incomplete and ineffective.

Who Are You "In Him"?

Notice that we are to count ourselves alive unto God *in Christ Jesus* (verse 11). Whenever you see phrases like "in Christ Jesus" or "in him" in the New Testament it's covenant phraseology. In other words, the passage is stating a fact about the believer who's in covenant with the Lord. Here's an example:

> **God made him who had no sin to be sin for us, so that <u>in him</u> we might become the <u>righteousness of God</u>.**
>
> **2 Corinthians 5:21**

Jesus didn't sin, of course, but the Father made him to be sin for us on the cross so that all those who enter into covenant with him would become the righteousness of God. The word 'become' in the Greek means to come into being, that is, to be born. Hence, we "become" the righteousness of God through spiritual rebirth. If you're a believer this means that **you are already righteous in your spirit** and therefore the more spirit-controlled you become the more righteous you will be.

The key to walking in *practical* righteousness is to be spirit-focused rather than flesh-focused because **you already are righteous in your spirit**. With this understanding, as you count yourself dead to sin make sure that you're also counting yourself alive to righteousness. It's the truth because it's who you already are in your spirit. Remember, Jesus said it's the truth that will set you free (John 8:31-32).

There are numerous ways the New Testament describes you in covenant with the LORD. While we already looked at positional truths in <u>Chapter Seven</u>, it's so vital that you understand **who you are** in Christ that they bear repeating. Here are ten ways the New Testament describes YOU:

1. You are **holy** (Colossians 1:21-22).
2. You are a **child of God** (John 1:12-13).
3. You are a **new creation** (2 Corinthians 5:17).
4. You are the **righteousness of God** (2 Corinthians 5:21).
5. You are **dead to sin** (Romans 6:11,14,18).
6. You are **more than a conqueror** (Romans 8:37).
7. You are a **temple of the Holy Spirit** (1 Corinthians 6:19-20)
8. You are **rich** (2 Corinthians 8:9).
9. You are **healed** (1 Peter 2:24).
10. You are a **royal priest** or **priestess** of the Most High God (1 Peter 2:9)!

These are all "positional truths." A positional truth is any truth from the Scriptures that reveals your *position* in covenant with God and therefore *how God sees you* because of this position. For instance, Colossians 1:22 declares that we are "holy **in His sight**, without blemish and free from accusation." This is **how God sees you** because this is *who you are* in Christ. Just be wise to repent when you miss it so that God can faithfully purify you from all unrighteousness (1 John 1:8-9). This is "keeping with repentance" (Matthew & Luke 3:8). Don't allow the build-up of unconfessed sin to block the power and favor of God in your life. A side benefit of this is that it keeps your heart soft and malleable rather than hard and incorrigible.

For the New Testament believer, meaning YOU, these ten descriptions reveal *who you are* in your spirit, the "new self" (Ephesians 4:22-24).

You practice these positional truths simply by **believing them and not disagreeing with them**. Remember, "The tongue has the power of life and death" so value and utilize this power accordingly. You must never speak words that contradict who God says you are. To so do would be like calling God a liar. Chew on these mind-blowing truths and any others you may find in the

Scriptures. **Meditate on them regularly and confess them**. The LORD lauded David as "a man after [His] own heart" (Acts 13:22). What was it that made David so praiseworthy? One thing for sure was that he earnestly meditated on God's Word:

> **I meditate on your precepts**
>> **and consider your ways.**
> **(16) I delight in your decrees;**
>> **I will not neglect your word.**
>>>> **Psalm 119:15-16**

The Hebrew for 'meditate' here is *siyach (SEE-ahk)*, which means "to ponder and converse with oneself and, hence, out loud." I encourage you to do this with positional truths. As you do, you'll grow in understanding and power. The more these truths become rooted in your heart, the more you'll be set free of the sinful nature and the more you'll soar in the spirit free of the limitations of carnality and the mundane.

Jesus said in John 8:31-32 that we must "continue" in his word if we are to "know the truth" and be set "free." Unlike your spiritual rebirth which happened instantaneously, your metamorphosis from caterpillar-thinking to butterfly-thinking is a *process*; it may not happen overnight, but it will happen, so don't give up. If you miss it, be quick to repent and God will forgive you, and then keep moving forward. You don't drown by falling in the water; you drown by staying in the water![23]

If all you do is change your thinking to focus on who you already are in your spirit—dead to sin, righteous, holy—you'll be blessed, but there are two other keys to participating in the divine nature and they have to do with your **body** and your **spirit.**

---

[23] For more details see the video "How God Sees YOU" at the Fountain of Life website or youtube.

2. Offering Your Body as a Living Sacrifice

Let's go back to Romans 6:11-12 and see what it goes on to say:

> **In the same way, count yourselves dead to sin but alive to God in Christ Jesus. (12) Therefore do not let sin reign in your mortal body so that you obey its evil desires. (13) Do not offer the parts of your body to sin, as instruments of wickedness, but rather <u>offer yourselves to God</u>, <u>as those who have been brought from death to life</u>; and <u>offer the parts of your body to him as instruments of righteousness</u>. (14) For sin shall not be your master, because you are not under law, but under grace.**
>
> **Romans 6:11-14**

Since we are dead to sin and alive to God in our spirits, Paul says that we shouldn't offer the parts of our bodies to sin as instruments of wickedness, but rather to God as instruments of righteousness. We can do this because we've been delivered from spiritual death to spiritual life, as verse 13 points out.

All unbelievers are spiritually dead. This doesn't mean they don't have a spirit and the capacity for good, but rather that their spirit is dead to God, which means that the ability to commune with the LORD doesn't exist. They're cut off from a relationship with their Creator because their spirit *cannot* connect or commune with him. Yet it's precisely because they have a spirit that they desperately want to connect with Him, even though it's impossible. This, of course, gives birth to religion, which is the human attempt to connect with God. Authentic Christianity, by contrast, is **God connecting with us** through spiritual rebirth in Christ by the Holy Spirit.

In this passage Paul reasons that, since we've been brought from a condition of spiritual death to spiritual life, we are to offer **the parts of our bodies** to God's service as instruments of righteousness. This refers to two things: **1.** Put into practice the truths you discover in God's Word, whether from your own studies or through receiving from others. In other words, line up your body with what God's Word teaches. This doesn't just include practical truths like "Husbands love your wives, just as Christ loved the church and gave himself up for her," but positional truths as well. How so? Because it takes your brain and your tongue to practice positional truth and both are parts of your body. If your brain and tongue aren't lining up with what God's Word says about you then you're not offering these parts of your body to Him as instruments of righteousness. **2.** Put into practice whatever instruction God gives you, which includes serving in any role He calls you to or moving toward any objective he gives you, as shown in <u>Chapter Six</u>: Seek the Lord in prayer concerning your purpose, both short-range and long-range. What are you inspired to do for God? What area of service really stirs you? Colossians 3:15 says to "let the peace of Christ rule in your hearts." What do you have a peace about doing? In other words, what do you have a good feeling about? Identify your strengths and then major in them. Grasp the unique task God has called you to do in each season of your life. Whatever it is, start doing it and ask for God's strength and direction. A journey of a thousand miles starts with the first step.

When you begin utilizing the parts of your body as instruments of righteousness in God's service the law of displacement comes into play. Light displaces darkness, righteousness displaces wickedness, spirit replaces flesh. Sin shall not be your master for you are not under law (legalism) but under grace (spirituality)!

A Living Sacrifice in Worship

There's even more to offering yourself to God:

> **Therefore, I urge you, brothers, in view of God's mercy, to <u>offer your bodies as living sacrifices</u>, holy and pleasing to God—<u>this is your spiritual act of worship</u>. (2) Do not conform any longer to the pattern of this world, but <u>be transformed by the renewing of your mind</u>. Then you will be able to test and approve what God's will is—his good, pleasing and perfect will.**
>
> **Romans 12:1-2**

This passage plainly details the first two steps to spirituality; that is, being spirit-controlled. Verse 2 instructs us to be transformed by the renewing of our minds, which we've already addressed. Verse 1 tells us to offer our bodies to God as "living sacrifices" and adds "this is your spiritual act of *worship*." 'Worship' means to "reverently honor or adore." We can worship in two ways: Through our actions and through our communion. Actions have to do with *practice*. When we sincerely practice the truths of God's Word we are also honoring the LORD, which is worship. It's the same thing when we start lining up our lives with His assignment, big or small, we're worshipping him. Either way, our actions give glory to God. Communion, however, has to do with *communication*. Prayer is communion with God and we specifically honor Him through the type of prayer known as praise & worship.

What exactly is praise & worship? The two go hand and hand. Praise is celebration and includes thanksgiving, raving and boasting; whereas worship is adoration. Praise naturally attracts God's presence and is in accordance with the law of respect: What you respect moves toward you while what you don't respect moves away from you. Worship, on the other hand, is adoration or awe, and is the response to being in His presence. See Psalm 95:1-7 and Psalm 100 for verification.

You'll see this principle at work in relationships all the time. Take, for instance, romantic relationships. Say if a woman is interested in a man and she praises his work, how will this make him feel? He'll feel important and respected. He'll feel like the "king of the world" and will naturally be more inclined to the woman, even if she's someone he might not have noticed otherwise. It's the same principle with God. When you start praising Him and boasting of Him He'll naturally be more inclined toward you. It's a simple principle.

In <u>Chapter Four</u> we observed that praise & worship can be further differentiated like so: Praise celebrates God whereas worship humbly reveres Him; praise lifts God up while worship bows when He is lifted; praise dances before God whereas worship pulls off His shoes; praise extols God for what He's done while worship adores Him for who He is; praise says "Praise the Lord" whereas worship demonstrates that He is Lord; praise is thanksgiving for being a co-heir in Christ while worship lays the crown at His feet.

Many believers are more comfortable with worshipping God through what they do rather than through communion, but I encourage you to excel in both. I run across a lot of wives who complain that their husbands rarely tell them that they love them, if ever. They hardly even compliment them. When confronted, the husband typically argues that he loves his wife by doing things for her, including working hard to bring home the bread. This is wonderful, of course, but the wife *still* wants to hear him communicate love to her. Do you think it's any different with God?

Some men tend to veer away from praise & worship because they think it's somehow girly. But, let me tell you something, David is one of the most passionate praise & worship warriors recorded in the Bible and he was wholly masculine. As a teenager he had the great faith and boldness to challenge the hulking Goliath with a slingshot when the entire army of Israel was shrinking back in terror (1 Samuel 17:24)! He went on to become one of the greatest kings of Israel, but God wouldn't allow him to build the temple because he was a warrior king and had too much blood on his hands! (See 1 Chronicles 28:3). Does this sound like a girly man? Or consider Moses' aide, Joshua. After Moses spoke with God in the Tent of Meeting, Joshua would stay and linger in God's presence (Exodus 33:11). Guess who God later chose to lead the Israelites in the conquest of Canaan? Joshua. There's clearly a link between those who choose to be mighty praise & worship warriors for God and those who are mighty warriors in his service. Those who are "ever praising" the LORD and who dwell in His presence "go from strength to strength" (Psalm 84:4-7). They are "transformed into his likeness with ever-increasing glory, which comes from the Lord, who is the Spirit" (2 Corinthians 3:18). In light of all this, anyone who claims that praise & worship is worthless or sissified is grossly ignorant.

Needless to say, every believer is called to deeper praise & worship. It will literally revolutionize your life, as it has mine and continues to do so.

If all we did was practice these first two keys to being spirit-controlled we'd be greatly blessed and experience freedom from the flesh to a higher degree than ever. But there's one more step and it has to do with our **spirit**. It's what the Bible calls praying in the spirit.

3. Praying in the Spirit and Charging Yourself Up

Let's look at a couple of key passages about praying in the spirit:

> **But you, dear friends, <u>build yourselves up</u>**
> **in your most holy faith and <u>pray in the Holy</u>**
> **<u>Spirit</u>.**
>
> **Jude 20**

This verse shows that believers in general should "build themselves up" in faith by praying in the Holy Spirit. It gives the impression of charging up our faith like a battery. In the Greek "build yourselves up" means "to build upon." You see, every believer has a measure of faith at the time of salvation (Romans 12:3), but this measure can be built upon as the believer grows. In other words, believers *should* increase in faith as they mature. How do we do this? One way is through God's Word (Romans 10:17), another is by spending time in God's presence through praise & worship; after all, God is full of faith and therefore those who hang around him will develop the same faith He has. It's the law of association. Jude 20 shows that praying in the Spirit is also essential for increasing in faith.

Here's another passage on praying in the spirit:

> **And <u>pray in the Spirit</u> <u>on all occasions</u>**
> **with all kinds of prayers and requests.**
>
> **Ephesians 6:18**

This verse appears right after Paul details the six pieces of the "armor of God," which shows that praying in the spirit is actually the seventh piece of the armor even though he doesn't analogize it like he does with the other six pieces (for instance, faith is a "shield" and the Word of God is a "sword" and so on). I liken praying in the spirit to *artillery* or a *missile* since you can pray in the spirit for people and situations a long distance away, even on the other side of the planet.

So we're clearly instructed in the Scriptures to charge up our faith by praying in the spirit and also to pray in the spirit on all occasions with all kinds of prayers and requests. The question now is, what is "praying in the Spirit"? After all, we can't very well pray in the spirit if we don't even know what it is. Thankfully, the Bible tells us exactly what it is:

> For **if I pray in a tongue, my spirit prays,** but my mind is unfruitful. (15) So what shall I do? **I will pray with my spirit**, but I will also **pray with my mind**; **I will sing with my spirit,** but I will also **sing with my mind.**
>
> **1 Corinthians 14:14-15**

By saying "if I pray in a tongue, my spirit prays" Paul was defining praying in the spirit. If he prayed in a tongue his spirit was praying, led of the Holy Spirit, and therefore he was praying in the spirit or praying in the Spirit (capitalized[24]). Praying in the spirit is synonymous with speaking in tongues, which is also known as glossolalia. What is speaking in tongues? It's when a believer prays from his spirit rather than his mind and therefore speaks in a language unknown to him. We see this in verse 15 where Paul notes two types of prayer—praying with his spirit and praying with his mind, singing with his spirit and singing with his mind.

Praying with your mind is obvious, it's praying with a language you understand, which is typically the language you most often speak. For me it would be English. When I pray in English I'm praying with my mind because it's a language I know and understand. Praying with one's mind is wonderful and this is usually what people think of when they think of prayer, but when we pray in this manner we are limited to our own understanding.

---

[24] Since there is no capitalization in the original Greek text translators have to determine if the word for spirit, *pneuma,* refers to the human spirit (un-capitalized) or the Holy Spirit (capitalized). Either/or works in this case since the human spirit prays as led of the Holy Spirit due to the fact that the believer's human spirit (un-capitalized) is birthed and indwelt by the Spirit (capitalized).

Whatever it is we're praying for—whether a person, people, place or situation—we're limited to our own understanding. This is where praying in the spirit comes into play. Praying in the spirit—speaking in tongues—bypasses the limitations of our understanding as led of the Holy Spirit. For instance, say if I'm praying for a believer who's struggling with a certain sin and has backslid to some degree. If I pray with my mind—my understanding—I am limited to what I know about the situation, but if I pray in the spirit for him I can address things beyond my understanding as led of the Holy Spirit. Or say if you're going to lose your job due to budget cuts or whatever in six months, but you don't know about it. You can't pray about this with your mind because you don't even know it's going to happen. But the Holy Spirit knows everything because He's God and indwells your spirit; He guides you. So when you pray in the spirit the Holy Spirit will likely guide your spirit to pray for your encouragement and a new job opportunity when you lose your current one in six months. You may not know about it, but the Holy Spirit does. As such, you were able to address something in prayer that your mind didn't even know about through praying in the spirit. In short, you bypassed the limitations of your understanding.

This is why Paul encouraged us to "pray in the Spirit on all occasions" in Ephesians 6:18 and it's why he stressed that he prayed and sung with both his mind and his spirit. *Both* are important.

The gift of personal tongues is for *all believers,* which is why these passages on praying in the spirit refer to all believers and not just to some who have a special gift. Note how none of these passages say anything like "Now, *if* you have the gift of tongues, pray in the spirit on all occasions" or "*If* you can speak in tongues build yourself up in faith by praying in the Holy Spirit." Back when these passages were written it was assumed that all believers had the gift of personal tongues. Virtually every believer had it because leaders in the church didn't shy away from emphasizing the importance of the baptism of the Holy Spirit, as they do today, unfortunately.

I describe praying in the spirit as "personal tongues" to distinguish it from the gift of tongues utilized in a church environment, which is followed by an interpretation in the common language. Not everyone has *this* gift, which Paul made clear in 1 Corinthians 12:30. The kind of speaking in tongues I'm talking about is different and refers to the believer praying *to God* with his or her spirit as led of the Holy Spirit. This is for *all* believers. Public tongues, on the other hand, isn't actually praying in the spirit because the believer who is functioning in this gift isn't praying *to God*, but is rather giving a message *from God* to the group of believers for their exhortation and encouragement. One refers to the believer praying to God with his/her spirit and the other refers to God speaking to the congregation. They're quite different. All believers can have the gift of personal tongues, but not all believers have the gift of public tongues. It's important to distinguish the two.

If every believer can have the gift of personal tongues, how do we get it? We receive it through the **baptism of the Holy Spirit**, which is covered in <u>Chapter Nine</u>.

Recapping the Three Keys to Walking in the Spirit

So the three keys to being spirit-controlled rather than flesh-ruled are as follows:

1. **Renew your mind.** Make it your mindset that you're dead to sin but alive to God in Christ Jesus. This includes making it your confession. Say: "I [state your name] am dead to sin and alive to God in Christ Jesus." Renewing your mind effectively includes lining up your thoughts and

words with who God's Word says you already are in Christ. For instance, the Bible says that you are dead to sin, holy, righteous and more than a conqueror in covenant with the Lord. These all describe who you are in your spirit as opposed to the flesh. You may not feel like you are these things, but you already are in your spirit. By accepting these positional truths by faith you're being spirit-focused rather than flesh-focused. Do it.

2. **Offer the parts of your body to God as instruments of righteousness.** This includes both serving the Lord—doing what God wants you to do (both general instructions from the Scriptures and specific instructions from the Spirit)—and praise & worship. Each of these puts into motion the law of displacement. By moving forward in the spirit you aren't slipping backwards in the flesh. By spending time in the light of God's presence through regular praise & worship darkness has no recourse but to flee. How do you get the darkness out of a room? You simply turn on the lights!

3. **Pray (and sing) in the spirit regularly.** This will keep you charged up and built-up in faith. It'll produce the power you need to walk in the full life Jesus came to give us; it'll empower you to love people you don't have warm feelings toward, including your enemies who hate you without cause. It'll enable you to walk in tough love when necessary, including righteous radicalness, like when Paul radically rebuked an arrogant sorcerer and temporarily cursed him with blindness to humble him, as led of the Holy Spirit (Acts 13:8-12). It'll provide the self-discipline necessary to overcome personal weaknesses, including lack of confidence, depression and various sin problems, like alcoholism, drugs, lying, gossip and slander.

Practicing these three principles is simply a matter of wisdom and love. The first and greatest command is to love God with all your heart and the second is to love people as you love yourself (Matthew 22:34-39). In a sense there are three commands since we are commanded to love others *as* we love ourselves, which means you have to love yourself first. I mean that in a healthy sense, of course, and not a narcissistic one. If you genuinely love yourself you'll put these principles into practice on a regular basis. After all, if you fail to implement them you won't have a victorious Christian life and you won't be intimate with God. You'll be encumbered and limited by personal weaknesses or areas of the flesh. This will not bless you, it won't bless those linked to you, and it won't bless God.

Practicing these three principles is the key to walking in the spirit or participating in the divine nature. It's the key to producing the fruit of the spirit and, therefore, being *spiritual* rather than *carnal*. Simply put, it's the key to being spirit-controlled rather than flesh-ruled. The former gives life while the latter brings death.

24/7 "God-Consciousness"

This is the key to having a vital, active relationship with God, which is the antidote to all forms of legalism. By "active relationship" I don't mean thinking about God once or twice a day, but rather 24/7 God-consciousness where you're **in constant connection and communion**. This makes sense of Paul's instruction to "pray without ceasing" in 1 Thessalonians 5:17 (KJV). How can anyone possibly "pray without ceasing"? By participating in the divine nature and walking in 24/7 God-consciousness. A close relationship with your heavenly Father requires the same time and attention that any close relationship requires. Like those relationships, it's not a chore, but a joy and an honor. It develops over time. David said, "Taste and see that the LORD is good" (Psalm 34:8). Once you've genuinely tasted of a relationship with God nothing else in life compares. It's the ultimate high!

It's your choice. You've been granted the awesome power of DECISION, which is volition. Whether you know it or not, you operated in this power to receive eternal salvation (Romans 10:9-10). Use this God-given gift to your advantage in your Christian walk. You're not a loser, you're a winner. Go forth and walk in the freedom and victory that God has bought for you at great cost! Rise up O man of God, rise up O woman of God, and soar on the heights in the spirit far above the limitations of the mental realm and the flesh! Amen.

"Put Off the Old Man"

One last exhortation before closing: It's imperative that you put off the "old man"—the flesh—for this to work. This is the very first thing we are instructed to do in Ephesians 4:22-24. We see the same instruction in this passage:

> **Do not lie to one another, since you have <u>put off the old man with his deeds</u>, (10) and have <u>put on the new man</u> who <u>is</u> renewed in knowledge according to the image of Him who created him,**
>
> **Colossians 3:9-10** (NKJV)

Before you can put on the new man—that is, effectively walk in the spirit—you have to be willing to put off the old man and "his" fleshly deeds. This means repenting of any area of the flesh once it is revealed to you as sin. You see, God deals with his children according to the light we have. Once we have revelation of something we are responsible for living according to it. See John 9:39-41 and 15:22 for verification. And, no, this isn't an excuse to stay in ignorance.

Let me give a widespread example. In modern Westernized cultures fornication is viewed as a normal lifestyle, but it's a sin according to God's Word. When the average male turns to the Lord he'll often come into the kingdom with the attitude that there's nothing wrong with fornication since it's such a widespread, accepted phenomenon. "Everyone does it," he might reason. As he grows spiritually, however, he comes to realize that it's wrong and God has something better for him. Up until this point God would automatically overlook transgressions in this area because he was corrupted by worldly culture and just didn't know any better. Once he *knows* the truth, however, he's obligated to walk according to it.

This is simply a matter of loving God, the first and greatest command (1 John 2:15-17). It's also a matter of wisdom or common sense. Yet I'm surprised at how many people refuse to give up fornication after becoming believers and discovering it's a sin. Then they wonder why they don't feel close to the LORD and they're not blessed. I'll tell you why—they're not putting off the old man! They're being stubborn and stupid.

Think about it like this: Say you're a parent and have a baby who soiled her diaper. You take the old diaper off, clean her up, and then put on the new diaper. Wouldn't it be absurd to put the new diaper over the old diaper? Yet this is what many Christians do in effect when they refuse to put off the old man before putting on the new. They try to put the new man over the old man and it doesn't work. No wonder they're frustrated!

So please be sure to put off the deceitful desires of the flesh by keeping in repentance.

We have a video at the Fountain of Life website that goes over the material in this chapter titled *How to Walk FREE of the Flesh*.

Twelve

Closing Word/Blessing

You now know what the Four Stages of Spiritual Growth are and you've likely located where you are spiritually and where you need to go. I encourage you to master the various principles relayed in <u>PART II</u>, apply them to your life and go on to spiritual maturity. Keep moving forward with God—*onward and upward!* (Proverbs 4:18).

May you know your Creator intimately and discern God's will as you seek Him first. May the Holy Spirit guide you as you take action to fulfill your God-given objectives in each area of life and each season. May you walk free of the flesh and soar in the spirit, producing the fruit thereof, fulfilling every good work and pleasing the LORD in every way.

Amen.

Bibliography

Brown, Francis/Driver, S.R./Briggs, Charles A. *Brown-Driver-Briggs Lexicon.* Peabody: Hendrickson Publishers, 1994

Bullinger, Ethelbert W. *A Critical Lexicon and Concordance to the English and Greek New Testament.* Grand Rapids: Zondervan Publishing House, 1975

Cameneti, Joseph. "How God Sees Us" (series). Believers Christian Fellowship, Warren, OH. September-October, 1986

Cameneti, Joseph. "Keys to Spiritual Maturity" (series). Believers Christian Fellowship, Warren, OH. February-March, 1996

Cameneti, Joseph. "Obtaining Your Desires II." Believers Christian Fellowship, Warren, OH. December 17, 1986

Cameneti, Joseph. "Walking Free from Sin" (series). Believers Christian Fellowship, Warren, OH. January-March, 1987

Coulter, Ann. *Godless: The Church of Liberalism.* New York: Crown Forum, 2006

Helps Word-Studies Lexicon. Retrieved from Biblehub.com. 1987, 2011

Lindsey, Hal. *There's a New World Coming.* New York: Bantam Books, 1973

Kirkwood, David. *Your Best Year Yet!* Pittsburgh: Ethnos Press, 1996

LORD, The. *English Standard Version (ESV). Holy Bible.* Chicago: Crossway, 2001

LORD, The. *King James Version. Holy Bible.* Iowa Falls: World Bible Publishers

LORD, The. *New American Standard Bible. Holy Bible.* Nashville: Holman, 1977

LORD, The. *New International Version. Holy Bible.* Nashville: Holman, 1986

LORD, The. *New International Version (Revised)*. *Holy Bible*. Nashville: Holman, 2011

LORD, The. *New King James Version Study Bible: Second Edition*. Nashville: Thomas Nelson, 2012

LORD, The. *New Living Translation*. Carol Stream: Tyndale House Publishers, 2006

LORD, The. *The Amplified Bible*. Grand Rapids: Zondervan, 1987

LORD, The. *Quest Study Bible: New International Version*. Grand Rapids: Zondervan, 2003

LORD, The. *World English Bible (WEB)*. Salt Lake City: Project Gutenberg, 2013

LORD, The. *Weymouth New Testament*. Ulan Press, 2012

LORD, The. *Young's Literal Translation (YLT)*. Grand Rapids: Baker Books, 1989

Peck, M. Scott. *The Different Drum*. New York: Touchstone, 1987

Peck, M. Scott. *Further Along the Road Less Traveled*. New York: Touchstone, 1993

Reagan, David. *God's Plan for the Ages: The Blueprint of Bible Prophecy*. McKinney: Lamb & Lion Ministries, 2005

Renner, Rick. *Seductive Spirits and Doctrines of Demons*. Tulsa: Rick Renner Ministries Inc. 1990

Servant, David. *Heaven Word Daily*. Pittsburgh: Ethnos Press, 2009

Savelle, Jerry. *In the Footsteps of a Prophet*. Crowley: Jerry Savelle Publications, 1999

Strandberg, Todd. *Defending the Pre-Trib Rapture*. Retrieved from https://www.raptureready.com/rr-pre-trib-rapture.html

Strong, James. *Strong's Exhaustive Concordance*. Grand Rapids: Baker, 1991

Vine, W.E. *Vine's Expository Dictionary of Biblical Words*. Cambridge: Nelson, 1985

Fountain of Life

Teaching Ministry

(Psalm 36:9)

The mission of Fountain of Life is to **set the captives FREE** by **reaching the world** with the **life-changing truths of God's Word**, the **power of the Holy Spirit** and the **Great News of the message of Jesus Christ**.

**We're calling Warriors all over the earth
to partner with us on this mission!**

Other Books by Dirk Waren:

The Believer's Guide to Forgiveness & Warfare (2012)
Legalism Unmasked (2013)
HELL KNOW! (2014)
SHEOL KNOW! (2015)

www.ingramcontent.com/pod-product-compliance
Lightning Source LLC
Chambersburg PA
CBHW071637050426
42443CB00026B/462